GARTH TURNER'S SURVIVAL GUIDE

GARTH TURNER'S SURVIVAL GUIDE

Personal Financial Planning for Canadians

Garth Turner

Summerhill Press
Toronto

Published by Summerhill Press, Toronto

Distributed by:
University of Toronto Press
5201 Dufferin Street
Downsview, Ontario M3H 5T8

Printed and bound in Canada

Canadian Cataloguing in Publication Data

Turner, Garth
Garth Turner's Survival guide

ISBN 0-920197-48-5

1. Finance, Personal - Canada. 2. Investments - Canada. I. Title. II. Title: Survival guide.

HG179.T87 1988 332.024'01'0971 C88-093617-7

Table of Contents

To the women in my life: Doris and Dorothy

Introduction

They don't tell employees the truth

This country is being run by people who want to enslave you.

Middle-class Canada is being systematically robbed of its dreams. The system is doing that. Zoning bylaws prohibit you from selling pies on your porch or lawn furniture from your garage. Your employer is forced by law to keep back a third of your salary for taxes. Banks and trust companies routinely throw out applications for small business loans unless they are 100 percent secured and totally without risk. The state is getting damn powerful. In Ontario employment equity legislation will force bosses to raise women's wages, even when they do different jobs than men. In Quebec, if it happens to be winter, a landlord can't evict a tenant who refuses to pay the rent.

Revenue Canada has awesome powers of search and seizure. Across most of Canada, rent controls make a total mess of the housing market. Municipal politicians, in many areas, seek to flex the ultimate muscle. Let me give you an example.

I own commercial real estate in a tourist town outside Toronto. Through the village of Campbellville rambles an historic roadway called the Guelph Line. At one end of town is the 401, Ontario's superexpressway leading to Metro Toronto. At the other, a dramatic climb onto the Niagara Escarpment. In early 1986 my wife, Dorothy, purchased another property—a Victorian red brick house—and renovated it into a Canadiana antique store. About a month later we asked the neighbors what they were doing with a tape measure across the road outside.

And so we heard of plans to widen the road, plans that would turn a meandering, tourist-pleasing village main street into an arterial roadway, plans that local authorities refused to make public until everything had been decided. I confronted regional road officials, who admitted to the project, asked me not to go public and said they regretted the leak of information. It was not democracy's finest hour. My response was to form a protest group, rouse the community through mass mailings and then hold a protest meeting carefully staged to attract maximum press coverage. One night in front of the village millpond I climbed atop bales of hay in the back of a pickup truck with four huge Canadian flags stuck in the holes where the side racks go. Several hundred people turned out, and it made for a wonderful clip on the evening television news.

Local officials were, as the saying goes, blown away. And in the end they agreed to let the community have input into the road plans while they were still at the development stage. It was, after a summer of wrangling with councillors and endless meetings, a fulfilling victory.

But it was not without blood. Resentful of the furor and the anti-government feelings I'd engendered, politicians at both the town and regional level struck out at me by seeking to close my wife's antique business. The bylaw enforcement officer would show up unannounced. Council would pass motions against us without notification. We were ordered to remove all our signs. We were told to rip off the steps leading to the front door. And in an historic hamlet with easily fifty technical encroachments along the main street, ours was the only one identified, then denied, by regional government. Again, action was taken at a meeting of which we were unaware. Again, we were ordered closed.

Finally, regional representatives were rolling up the driveway of our farm, threatening to take more action. The last straw came when the Region of Halton ordered a sign at the end of our laneway—a sign that identified our residence—removed because it encroached on regional land. On a twenty-mile stretch of roadway, where scores of similar signs existed, this was the only instance of enforcement. But we did not give in. It meant threatening to take the regional chairman to the Ontario Municipal Board. It involved appearing before intensely hostile local councillors. It meant a steady stream of outraged letters to area newspapers. And, sadly, it meant devoting precious business time to petty political broadsides from people it became impossible to respect. It is not over yet, but more harassment will be met with a suit citing Canada's Charter of Rights. You cannot seek to quell a man's right to free speech in this country by using political blackmail. Singling out minute bylaw infractions for one business while choosing to ignore all the others that exist in a municipality clearly contravenes the charter's concept of equality. So the fight does not end.

This garbage is all too indicative of the direction society is headed in this country. We give lip service to free speech, but it makes us uncomfortable. We say we are a capitalist society, and yet we give over to government far too much control of the business environment. We have grown to see our financial institutions rip us off; we don't trust the men and women we elect; and there are deep divisions between labor and management. How many major strikes have there been in the past year? How has a confrontational leader like Bob White of the Canadian Auto Workers become a kind of folk hero?

Canada is great and it is good. But it is also being squandered. We take the easy way out, continuing to pump oil, sell fish and cut trees. After twelve decades of nationhood we are still resource-based, strung out in a thin line along the southern border and happy to work for big government.

Big changes are taking place. The old folks want the government to support them. The yuppies measure life more by possessions than by the personal independence that comes from the control of financial assets. The kids coming up behind them are walking into an era of absolute turmoil. The country is bankrupt; our American brother is in decline and decay despite desperate attempts to compete; the wealth base of the globe is shifting daily to Japan; and we are in for some financial upheavals that will make Black Monday—Oct.19, 1987—look quaint by comparison.

In a world like this, you need the freedom to call your own shots. You need to guard against recession, when employers turn tough and lay people off so the company can survive. What's good for the corporation may not be good for all the employees; a reorganization can help the balance sheet, but it lays waste the lives of middle managers who are shown the door in the name of efficiency. You need as well the ability to survive the whims of others. Maybe it's the person who's your immediate superior. Maybe it's the untrusting bank manager. Maybe it's those around you who are lazy and jealous. To manage this, friends, you need guts, a taste for hard work, the willingness to take risks and, most important, the ability to rise above the slipping norms of the country you live in.

Face it: employees don't make it. They are never allowed to be free because their freedom is not in the best interests of their employer. Instead, "successful" employees are trapped with just enough wealth to become dependent on their paycheques. They are tricked into thinking their identity is tied up in their job title. And at the end, they're left with an inadequate pension, a vaporized circle of office "friends" and a life in its fourth quarter.

Employees don't make it. Managers don't make it. Even vice-presidents don't make it.

But risk-takers do. Entrepreneurs do. Investors do. Owners do.

Take your choice. Choose the typical middle-class Canadian way and be an at-risk, career employee. Or choose the path to personal financial independence.

As I write, my wife and I are trying to progress along that path. In the twelve months from December 1986, our net worth increased by just over $1 million. I am not bragging, but rather trying to show that a regular guy holding down a full-time job can do a lot more for himself than get addicted to a paycheque. He can get personal satisfaction along the way. And he can get independence.

So, where did I get that money?

Most of it came from playing around in the real estate market. But it also came from residential construction, the operation of a mail-order company, a retail business, public seminars, precious metals and stocks.

My bank manager routinely offers me a $200,000 personal line of credit. I drive a Mercedes. My wife drives one, too. (We're not without our weaknesses for yuppie goods.) We live on a $600,000 property. In late 1987 we added a $120,000 extension to our house. And paid for it with cash.

I am thirty-nine years old. When I was thirty-seven my net worth was maybe $250,000. In two years it is five times that.

All this happened because I decided to get serious about my financial freedom. Four years ago both my wife and I were employees of large companies. We were managers, earning over $40,000 each, with generous benefit packages, bonuses and stock purchase plans. Dorothy had a big office and a personal secretary. She ran a department with maybe a dozen employees, wore power suits and went from one meeting to another. I had turned down promotions because they would do nothing but lead to corporate entrapment—and more paycheque addiction. I was on an executive bonus plan and wrote a column read by two hundred thousand people. We were both successful (within a fairly narrowly defined context), working at the top of our industries, in a competitive environment, in a city of three million people.

But we were going nowhere. Each day was like the one before. One week was like the next. One year's experience was a close rerun of the one before. Worse, we had the nagging feeling that, as employees, we were trading away the one thing we could not replace: time. Surely we could have both time and money. We decided on a plan—a plan to escape financial dependence on others and on corporate circumstances we could not control.

This was not the first time in our marriage that we had quested to be free. Ten years earlier, still in our twenties, we borrowed $40,000 and started a newspaper with eight employees. We had enough money to last for eight weeks, and we prayed for cash flow to take over from there. Three years later we sold the company for a lot of money. At that time we had four newspapers and sixty employees.

Dorothy and I have been married for seventeen years. At first we went to university by day and I parked cars at night. We lived in a desperate little apartment with windows fifteen feet from an elevated rapid transit line. We were robbed there. We allocated one dollar a day for food for both of us. In the summer I worked for a brewery and smuggled home two bottles of beer each night. We bought our first car for $400, and Dorothy drove it fifty miles to her first teaching assignment—in the wrong gear.

I quit university in graduate school and had to give back the only money we had, a $3,000 scholarship. I found a job writing editorials for a little daily newspaper in Oakville, Ontario. The pay was $100 a week. Dorothy finished school a hundred miles away. It was terrible leaving each other every week. It was wonderful coming back.

We are middle-class people. Our parents are not wealthy. There was no deep pool of money to dip into when the going got rough. But there was a deeply instilled and important set of values that included a reverence for work and a knowledge that we had to live within our means.

Over the years we have tried many things. We have made mistakes. We've lucked into some great deals. Sometimes we have bounced around too fast. Sometimes we waited too long to act. Along the way we have learned that it is not a bad thing to challenge authority.

It is not wrong to quit your job, so long as you have your sights set on that path to personal financial independence. It's not poor planning to go deeply in debt, so long as it's the right kind of debt and it gets you something meaningful in return. It really is true that you make it by buying low and selling high. And that's exactly why the consumption-driven yuppies are one of the most enslaved generations in history.

Anyone who has not listened to the cracks opening in the earth probably deserves their fate. After Black Monday, for example, life should have changed for most people. I don't care if you had money in the stock market or not—this was a warning sign of massive proportions. The financial order is changing. By the time this book gets into your hands we could be headed for a recession. Then layoffs will be the order of the day and the enslaved will be asking the government to "do something."

But the emperor is starkers. The feds are broke. The provinces are overextended. America may be the world's biggest debtor nation but, on a per capita basis, Canada is even more deeply in debt. The time has never been better for people of vision to start thinking about where they are on the path. Personal financial independence—freedom—that's the goal.

We're not really talking about RRSPs here, as useful as they may be to slice through some taxes. This is not a book about term deposits or how to spend fifteen hours each April saving two hundred bucks on your tax return. The shelves are full of that stuff, and a bunch of such books are listed for you in chapter four.

I'm not going to tell you to put your money in the banks and trust companies in return for a few shreds of (now taxable) interest. Instead, let's talk about taking that money yourself, making it grow and then reaping the benefits. Let's talk about tax reform, real estate, cash investments, gold and silver, T-bills and American bank accounts. After all, this book is about giving life a twirl.

Chapter One

The middle class vs. the economy

The people most at risk in Canada are those who belong to the middle class.

Let's use Finance Minister Mike Wilson's own description of who these folks are: those with a family income of between $27,500 and $50,000. Under tax reform, they will carry the greatest load, with a tax rate almost 50 percent higher than lower-earners' and just 9 percent less than people making big bucks.

Of course, you can earn $70,000 and still be middle class. Anybody who labors for a paycheque, has taxes lopped off at source and then has to make do in an after-tax, inflationary world is in roughly the same boat. Whether you work on the line at General Motors or you're vice-president of an advertising agency, you're still at risk from several factors you can neither influence nor control.

Because it's important to know your enemies, take a good, close look at some of those factors, namely inflation, the dollar, interest rates, taxation, and deficits and the national debt.

Inflation

This seems like a permanent part of the economy. We really suffered in the 1970s and compared with the double-digit levels endured then, today's 5 percent or so seems like no big deal.

But it is.

The official inflation figure released monthly by Statistics Canada is highly misleading. For example, house prices went up about 40 percent across most of southern Ontario last year. Food costs were up nationally more that 5 percent, just like car insurance rates and bank service charges. Meanwhile average wage gains were less than 3 percent. Hell, some workers went on strike to get packages promising 10 percent raises *over three years*. That would have been laughable when this decade began.

The point is that a great number of middle-class workers are being bullied into a poorer standard of living. Inflation protection is essentially gone from the workplace. And it is also gone from taxation now. With wage gains less than inflation, people are falling a lot further behind than they realize. This partly explains why savings accounts have been raided over the past eighteen months, while bank loans and mortgages have been ballooning.

Inflation is still a very real and menacing threat. Anyone who settles—without a struggle—for an annual wage gain of less than the prevailing rise in the consumer price index had better be ready to cut their spending pattern. Otherwise they lose.

Inflation, by the way, is going to get a lot worse before it gets better.

The first thing that central banks did after the stock market crash of October 1987 was pump gobs of money into the financial system. A number of important U.S. investment banks were in serious trouble.

Canadian investment companies were also in desperately condition. Even some of the big banks and trust companies wondered what they were going to do for liquidity. Suddenly central banks threw away the tight-money policies they'd been following. They went from worrying about the money supply increasing too quickly (which would mean each dollar was worth less—which is inflation) to making sure the printing presses were humming.

When the choice came between more inflation and a meltdown in the financial markets, the central banks chose the first. The long-term consequence of printing all this money is inevitable: prices will go higher faster. People in multiyear contracts, with less than 5 percent promised in each, are going to wish their union leaders had more vision.

The Dollar

We haven't had a real dollar crisis for a couple of years, not since the buck bottomed around the 69-cent U.S. mark. Our currency has been more or less steady in the 75- to-77-cent range, and government officials have taken some comfort in emphasizing that stability.

What they fail to mention, however, is that the American greenback has suffered one of the most severe devaluations in history. Against the Japanese yen and the West German mark, the U.S. dollar has never before been worth less. So, as our dollar stays "stable," or even rises, against theirs, we are actually riding the escalator down against the rest of the industrialized world.

Now, this is good and it is bad. A cheapo buck makes our exports look less expensive to foreign buyers, and so we stand a better chance of trading our goods for much-welcomed cash. Canada is a trade-dependent nation. We have very expensive tastes and too small a domestic market to support them. We badly need those foreign sales.

This low-valued Canadian currency also makes other things look like bargains to people with foreign cash to burn. Like real estate. More on this later, but by world standards our land is an absolute steal. Middle-class Japanese, for example, stand about a zero chance of finding affordable housing in Tokyo. A two-bedroom condo an hour and a half away sells for a tad less than $300,000. But the average house in Canada's biggest city, maybe fifteen minutes from downtown, can still be had for little more than $200,000. An hour away the same amount of money could buy you two houses. Canadian real estate is undervalued, and the rest of the world is starting to notice.

In December of 1986 I bought an investment property for $370,000. It about doubled in value over the next year as a real estate boom raged locally. But I was not prepared one day when a guy representing Hong Kong investors tried to buy it—for a million dollars. I didn't need the cash, and I didn't sell. Give me a couple of more years, as the Chinese takeover of Hong Kong grows closer, and the price will be even better.

Okay, so our low dollar creates some interesting possibilities. But it can also create problems. When your wealth is trapped in a declining currency, it stands to reason you are losing money. Think about the poor middle-class people in Brazil, Mexico, Argentina, Peru, the Philippines and other countries where economic mismanagement has seriously devalued the local currency. In some countries citizens are prohibited from sending money out of the country, or from converting it into something more valuable, like American dollars.

In these countries people who kept all their wealth in local currencies lost it. Those who saw the troubles coming took some action. They took money across the border and converted it. They got rid of paper and instead bought real estate. Or they went for the security of something eternal, like gold. And they were the survivors.

Most Canadians don't believe we could suffer the same economic nightmares that these debtor countries have experienced. But it's entirely possible that we could.

Canada is deeply in debt, and getting more so. Our dollar has declined largely because of our debt. The government pays lip service to fixing this problem but takes no real action unless there's an immediate crisis. Imagine, for example, if an NDP government took office. International money traders would greet the prospect of a socialist government in Canada by selling out our currency. The buck could slip to 50 cents, prompting average Canadians to panic and start opening up bank accounts in border-point American banks. Prime Minister Broadbent would likely respond to this serious hemorrhaging of capital by imposing currency controls. Suddenly we would be in a pitiful situation. Your wealth would be trapped in an eroding currency.

Folly? I don't think so. I think it could happen.

Interest Rates

This is another area where fallout from a sick buck can do a lot of damage. Because Canada is so much in debt, we can no longer set our own interest rates. I mean, the finance minister can't stand up in Parliament one day and announce that the Bank of Canada rate will be pegged at 3 percent. They can do that in Tokyo and Bonn, but not in Ottawa.

The difference is that Japan and Germany are creditor nations. The world owes them, their banks, their investment dealers and their citizens more than they owe foreigners. So their interest rates are set for reasons other than to attract investment capital.

Not with us, however. Canada and the United States, are net debtor nations. That means we owe money—piles of the stuff—to other countries. In order to make these debt payments while raising enough money to run the country, we have to gain new investment dollars. One way of doing this is to set high interest rates so those foreign investors will be attracted here where they can get a good rate of return.

So this prevents the finance minister from just chopping rates. If the minister *did* do this, then we'd have a problem financing our national cash requirements, and the value of the dollar would quickly be traded down on money markets.

If you want to know the direction of short-term interest rates, then keep an eye at all times on the dollar. If it starts to slip, the Bank of Canada reacts immediately. Every Thursday afternoon at two o'clock the big bank auctions off a mess of little bonds in Ottawa, and the yield it receives determines rates for that week. The week the dollar goes down is the one when rates go up.

Interest rates are incredibly important. When they're low, people borrow and the economy gets fuelled. High rates were one big reason we had the 1982 recession. You'll remember that's when people were facing mortgage renewals of 21 percent and more, which had the devastating effect of doubling monthly payments. The rates were high because we had to follow the

American model of rising money costs. The Americans were doing it under the direction of chief central banker Paul Volcker in an attempt to cool out the economy and lower inflation. The policy worked, and within a year or so Americans had a zero inflation rate. Of course, *we* also had a lousy economy and tons of unemployment.

This inflicted a lot of hardship on individuals. The combination of high interest and much joblessness showed many people that they had been ill-prepared for any kind of downturn in the economy. Yet in several ways we were better prepared for trouble then than we are now. Personal savings were higher and household debt was lower. If similar circumstances hit today, the Canadian middle class would be dead meat.

I went to Ottawa in 1981 when mortgages were 20 percent. I took with me over a thousand people and, as I recall, more than twenty buses. This trip came after a series of my newspaper columns ripped into the feds for not managing the rate crisis better. The Trudeau government was simply letting homeowners twist in the wind. But

Gathering on the side of the highway fifty miles out of Ottawa, part of the convoy of buses waits for other vehicles to rendezvous. Inside are hundreds of Canadians going to Parliament Hill to protest high interest rates. My columns against the government's policies led to this event, along with an eventual moratorium on home foreclosures.

those were precisely the people who couldn't insulate themselves from crazy interest rates, and obviously needed protection.

When we reached Parliament Hill, we were greeted by a wall of RCMP officers in full riot gear. You know the stuff—helmets with visors, clubs and those plastic shields you can see through. The same kind of outfit you see on T.V. as rocks and firebombs hit the streets of Manila.

These forces prevented our group from getting into our own Parliament buildings. Finally the minister of state responsible for housing, Paul Cosgrove, agreed to see a small number of us. And that night he announced a moratorium on all bank and trust company foreclosures resulting from high interest rates.

To a large extent, interest rates rule the economy. When five-year mortgage rates bottomed out at 10 percent in the spring of 1987, several Canadian markets saw the hottest real estate boom in two generations. It also fuelled car sales and business investment. It helped the economy spurt ahead at a crucial time—six months before the confusion and gripping losses of Black Monday.

But low rates were the scourge of inves-

RCMP in full riot gear gave a warm welcome to the seat of government. Busloads of middle-class Canadians who had never seen anything like this before learned a lesson in participatory democracy. So did I.

tors. "Investment-grade" savings accounts—some of them requiring a balance of at least $50,000—were paying barely more than the inflation rate. Getting a decent rate of return on cash investments has not been easy for many months. But it is still possible.

As short-term rates rise, one of the best places to be is in Treasury bills. These fully guaranteed government bonds are available only from an investment dealer, not a bank or trust company (so don't be fooled by one that offers a "T-bill account"). They are available in terms as short as ninety days, so you don't need to tie your money up for a long period of time. And they carry a far higher rate of return than you can get at the bank. Plus, you get your interest up front when you buy because T-bills are sold on a discounted basis. If a $10,000 bill is paying 8 percent, for example, you buy it for less than its face value. The discount is equal to the amount of interest that investment would earn over the term you choose.

Another good way to get a better rate of interest is with a mortgage-backed security, or MBS. Here we have the perfect marriage of yield and quality. This type of investment has been available in the United States since the early 1970s, but only in Canada since the beginning of 1987. And it has caught on big—although far too few Canadians yet know about Cannie Maes. That's what these new bonds are called because they copy the American security created by the Government National Mortgage Association, or GNMA, or Ginnie Mae. This may all be hopelessly cutesy, but Cannie Maes are worth looking into.

For starters, there is little safer to invest in than residential first mortgages. A mortgage is a loan secured by a piece of property. If the guy owning the land fails to make payments on the loan, then the lender can take over the asset. In a country where real estate values have marched higher year after year, this is obviously a good deal.

Now, imagine an investment that sends you cheques every month like clockwork. Imagine getting a return of 10 percent or better, guaranteed for five or ten years. Imagine absolutely no risk, a government guarantee and an investment that could never backfire. Imagine something you could get into with relatively little money. And finally, imagine an investment that was also liquid, allowing you to sell whenever you wanted—maybe even at a premium if interest rates had declined since you bought it. Well, that's what a Cannie Mae is all about.

This relatively new investment vehicle was launched by the Canada Mortgage and Housing Corporation (CMHC) to raise more money for housing and to try to stabilize long-term mortgage rates. The idea was to give investors a good rate of return and a guaranteed security. In the States, Ginnie Maes have created a steady flow of real estate funds and have allowed homeowners to have ten-, fifteen- or twenty-year mortgages at fixed rates. They've also given investors a secure source of monthly income and the freedom to cash out when they want to.

The idea is simple: A bank or trust company bundles up a bunch of its existing residential mortgages and then gets together with an investment house (like Merrill Lynch, Dominion Securities, Wood Gundy, McLeod Young Weir and so on). They create a Cannie Mae: a security backed by those mortgages. The shares are sold to investors in units of $5,000 each. People who buy these units are given a certificate by a central transfer agent showing the amount invested. As I said, because the securities are backed by mortgages, there is very little risk involved. But to eliminate whatever risk might be left, CMHC guarantees that investors will always get their money back.

Okay, so a return of 10 percent and no risk. Sounds great. But there's even more to Cannie Maes. This is what's known as a modified pass-through mortgage-backed security. In human talk that means it pays you a regular income. Investors get all payments on principal, prepayments and interest.

Think of it this way: When you make a payment on your mortgage, that money goes to the bank that lent you the cash in the first place. But imagine if the bank sold your mortgage to somebody else, because it didn't want to wait forever to get its money back. Then your payments would flow to this new person, who might well be a Cannie Mae investor. So that guy would be getting a regular income from you. Each Cannie Mae pays investors a steady monthly income, on the fifteenth day, starting forty-four days after the issue date of the MBS offering. And this cash flow is guaranteed in case of default by the mortgagee.

The money you invest in a MBS is generally tied up for five years, though a secondary market is developing among people interested in buying already-issued Cannie Maes. Usually they think interest rates are going in a certain direction, which will make these investment attractive to them. For you it means a lot more liquidity than you'd have with, say, a guaranteed investment certificate (which does not send you a monthly cheque). On the secondary market, if interest rates drop, then you sell out at a premium. If they rise, you take a loss, just like with mortgage mutual funds.

Contact a broker and find out when the next MBS offering may be. Some of the investment houses that have been most active in this field are Dominion Securities, Richardson Greenshields, Merrill Lynch, Levesque Beaubien, McLeod Young Weir and Wood Gundy.

One last point: Cannie Mae can be put inside an RRSP, so the regular income you receive is sheltered from tax. This makes it an ideal tool for building retirement money. It is also an excellent investment for retired people looking for a secure, safe, regular monthly income. By the way, one of the first MBS offerings was comprised of Canada Trust mortgages. In early 1987 it offered a Cannie Mae paying 11.5 percent on a ten-year term, which today looks pretty impressive.

So, you ask , why is it that something paying a good return, offering regular monthly payments and 100 percent risk-free is something you probably never heard of? And why is it that most average Canadians have no idea what a Treasury bill is, even though it, too, is high-yield and worry-free?

Because these are financial products that the banks and the trust companies and the credit unions don't offer. To invest in things like this, you have to go to an investment house. Many Canadians link this with a stock market investment and, lately, that scares the heck out of them. Too bad. There's some good stuff out there.

But this is going to change—and change very soon. Ottawa recently relaxed some of the rules governing the money business. One of those had prevented banks and trust companies from owning investment houses. Now all the major banks have forged relationships, and we are well on the way to one-stop financial shopping.

The day is not far off when you'll be able to buy Cannie Mae units in the same place where you pay your Visa bill, buy a mortgage, keep a chequing account and get cash for groceries. It will be a stunning new development, and a better system.

Taxation

Diverted momentarily, but now back on track, here is another mortal threat to your wealth. In fact, this is the worst. It is a lot harder to earn a buck than it is to save one. And a dollar saved is really more important than one earned because you have to fork out typically between 25 and 40 cents of each new dollar for taxes.

This makes tax planning very important. The trouble is, however, that tax reform—in effect since January 1, 1988—severely cuts down on the ways you might have of legally avoiding taxation. Most exemptions and deductions have been turned into credits, and the net effect is to stick it in the ear of the middle wage-earner. This is especially true in my case, a married taxpayer without children. Last-minute changes to Mike Wilson's tax reform paper came out light on big families.

More on tax reform later. Right now it's enough to say that the government's total tax take over 1988 and 1989 is scheduled to increase by about $5 billion. Taxes are higher on almost everything, from a bottle of my favorite scotch to kitty litter and wallpaper. The myth of tax reform is that it will put more money into your pocket. The reality is that the slight increase in your take-home pay will be eaten up by higher consumer product and service prices. When stage two of tax reform takes effect—a new, broad-based national sales tax—things will get vastly worse. The sales tax rate could be between 8 percent and 10 percent, and apply to everything you buy, with the exception of food and drugs.

In the first three years of the Mulroney Tory government, direct and indirect personal taxation just about exactly doubled. It is the country's chief growth industry. Many Canadians haven't noticed it because these years have also been ones of robust economic growth, marked by rampant consumerism and accompanied by runaway stock markets.

But that's not to say the tax romp doesn't hurt. A couple of federal budgets ago I used my newspaper column to ask people how they felt about massive tax hikes just unveiled by Mike Wilson. I ran a little coupon at the bottom of the column and was stunned when forty-thousand responses poured in.

Naturally, I went back to Ottawa to dump this evidence of middle-class disgust in the lap of the finance minister. A representative group of ten or twelve readers came along to share the experience, and we found ourselves dragging sacks of coupons up the steps of Parliament Hill. This time there were no RCMP storm troopers, which was a nice departure from the Trudeau days. No, this time there were just a handful of beaver-brained security guards who insisted the bags could not be carried through the front door.

Followed by television crews, we tried the side door, and finally ended up waiting in a room at the back, close to the garbage dumpsters. After debate, hassle and intimidation, the coupons ended up in a big red plastic cart, which we wheeled through the corridors of power.

Wilson didn't get them—sadly, he was out of the country. But the junior finance minister, Barbara MacDougall, did. She also was forced to sit in her office and listen to a bunch of average Canadian working stiffs take a round out of her government. I think it was a good experience for everyone.

The red plastic cart, filled with forty thousand letters from readers who objected to yet another round of federal tax increases. Finance Minister Mike Wilson didn't want to see me, but Liberal leader John Turner (no relation) was all too happy with the media attention. I'm in the middle. The guy on the right is Toronto dentist Steve Starkman, a staunch defender of capitalism (aren't all dentists?) and one of the readers who helped me haul those letters to the House of Commons.

But taxes did not drop. Instead we got tax reform, which sets the stage for revenue increases in the future.

The basic problem here is that Canadians have been shackled with governments that cannot stop spending. Increased demands on the system mean they either go back and tax again or they borrow more from domestic and international investors. Lately, governments have been in the habit of doing both at the same time. During a period of economic expansion, you can get away with that kind of garbage. When a recession looms, you can't. During bad times, the tax base falls as individuals lose their jobs and as corporations stop making profits. By increasing taxes, government risks turning a recession into a depression. And during periods like these, the deficit swells as government is forced to spend more on things like unemployment insurance payments. This brings us to:

Deficits and the National Debt

There is a difference, you know, although most people kind of lump them together.

Each year the Government of Canada spends more money than it raises in taxes. This is called the budgetary deficit, and in the 1988/89 fiscal year the deficit will be roughly $29 billion.

We're not the only country to do this, by any means. The United States also runs a budget deficit, and it also is out of control. But at about $190 billion a year, it is far less terrifying, on a per capita basis, than Canada's. Remember, too, that international concern about this deficit was so great in late 1987 that it helped cause the worst stock market crash in history. The White House response was to cut a deal with Congress that would reduce the deficit by $76 billion over two years—which was clearly too little and far too late.

Now, the deficit that Canada runs each

year is financed by borrowings. Some of the money is borrowed from us, in the form of Canada Savings Bonds. Some of it is borrowed from large investors who buy Government of Canada bonds. These borrowings each year are then added to the national debt. Right now that debt is about $260 billion, and growing fast. Tax reform documents tabled in the summer of 1987 reveal that the debt will be more than $400 billion by 1991. And that's if nothing goes wrong. It assumes no recession, good economic growth, high commodity prices, low interest rates and no jumps in unemployment In short, the estimate is probably not worth the powder to blow it up—our debt load will be far greater. And this is a national tragedy.

Right now it takes almost $28 billion a year to pay the interest on the outstanding debt. Each year we have to borrow that whole amount (and more), and so the debt the next year is that much bigger. Right now it takes over a third of all taxes collected to pay this interest, which seems like a hell of a waste of good dollars. By the 1990s this could rise to more than 40 percent of taxes collected, and the government will still be handcuffed by its debt obligation. You don't hear much about this, do you?

The Trudeau years left us with a terrible legacy—a $38 billion deficit in 1983/84, following the 1982 recession. The Mulroney Tories came to power saying that deficit reduction was a primary goal and that Canada was on "a dangerous treadmill." Well, we're still on it. In fact, the speed has been turned up as we trot toward destruction. In the first three years of this administration, our national debt increased by over $100 billion. The amount of cash we must raise every year to finance this debt doubled. So did taxation. And now the goal of deficit reduction is clearly on the back of the policy stove.

We are still running annual deficits of close to $30 billion—and these have been good economic times, times when a responsible government would want to be storing for the lean years. As I told you, tax reform spells out clearly that our debt will soon be over $400 billion. In their final year of office, the Conservatives have backed off the slogan we once heard—short-term pain for long-term gain.

Many Canadians apparently think that's just fine. Which is why the deficit and the national debt are not political issues. They will likely not even be raised in the coming federal election. Certainly the Liberals and the New Democrats are not going to espouse chopping social spending programs in order to reduce our financial requirements. In fact, both parties are on record as saying we need to spend more. More on a national daycare program,more on health care, more on education and transfer payments to the provinces and more on culture.

Because most Canadians apparently agree with many of those objectives, and because most of us don't know what a time bomb we're assembling with every new buck borrowed, the politicians don't tell us. We don't know that Canada goes into debt another $60,000 every minute. We have a great debate about the threat of free trade to our sovereignty while we allow a massive and unrepayable mortgage to be placed on our nation. This is sheer hypocrisy on the part of those who should know better.

The implications of this national delusion are great. Immediately it means that taxes will continue to rise while the Canadian dollar lives a day-to-day existence. Interest rates will remain volatile, and we will continue to be impotent in setting our own monetary agenda. Whatever head

U.S. central banker Alan Greenspan does, Bank of Canada boss John Crow will ape, probably within a few hours. We will continue to swim in the backwash of the American economic empire, which is in serious trouble.

In the long term your children and your grandchildren will wonder how they came to inherit such a mess. How, they'll ask, did Canadians come to screw things up so badly during the 1980s? How did we go from a reasonably balanced budget at the beginning of the decade to a debt of $400 billion by the end? What, exactly, did we get for it?

The reality is that Canada currently enjoys a lifestyle that it cannot afford. With our level of income it's crazy to think we can, as a society, impose pay equity laws, provide subsidized rental housing for the middle class, have the state assume responsibility for child-rearing or pay people for getting old. Social compassion has turned into excess. We debate a guaranteed annual income. We pay people not to work. We have compensation benefits so generous that injured workers don't want to go back on the job. You don't believe that? Well, the Ontario Workers' Compensation Board now pays pensions to workers who say they have imagined pain, an injury that cannot be medically proven. And even injuries sustained off the job are eligible for employer-paid benefits. The board, by the way, has awarded about $6 billion more than it has funds to pay out. That money will be torn from the hide of business in the form of ever-rising annual dues.

North America is losing it. The work ethic is an endangered moral. The rapid and massive accumulation of debt on this continent is proof that we're no longer willing to wait for the spoils of wealth, or to work for them. Many people say this attitude has been most refined in the people we call yuppies. Yuppie started out as a term for young, urban professionals, but now it's synonymous with mindless consumption, consumerism and the conspicuous display of material possessions. It means a taste for designer clothes, luxury cars, specialty foods and $300,000 near-suburban four-bedroom Georgian replicas. All this comes with a big mortgage, a fat personal line of credit and a purse full of gold credit cards. And if that's not *your* lifestyle, it sure is the one made glamorous by the media.

Everything's cool while the cash flow is good, but when it's interrupted—by something as big as social change or as small as a recession—the imbalance of debt to equity is crushing. Each day that Canada as a nation acts like a yuppie, this generation is at risk. We heighten the chances of a severe economic downturn as we lose the ability to set our own policies or agendas.

Things are a lot more fragile than they appear. You are not getting the whole story from the people you elected. And you have reason to fear the future if you are also excessive in your own life. If you get nothing else out of this book, get this: the very best investment you can make is to reduce your personal level of debt. The key to survival is to do what your country is not doing. Be responsible in your budget and in your spending. If the feds don't have the courage and visions to live within their means, then you must.

I'm not saying you should go and hide under a rock. But I am saying it is essential that you consider launching out on a plan that will make you, in a year or three or five, debt-free. Consider things like a weekly mortgage, which will pay off your home loan in roughly half the time of a conventional loan. Make sure you operate out of cash flow instead of borrowings. Take a hard look at the rate of return you are getting on your savings, because unless it's spectacular you're a lot better off using this money to pay down debt.

Given the actions of government, the constant borrowing, the inability to slash spending, the kneejerk capitulation to special interest groups—seniors, women, ethnic groups (sorry, folks, this probably includes one you're part of)—we are on a long-term collision course with Trouble. Recession and job loss are in the cards—it's just a matter of timing. The current business cycle is coming to an end, and we can see some of that trouble start to take hold. More likely, however, are a few more years of denial and self-deception on this continent. Central banks will tinker with the money supply. Governments will find more creative ways to borrow money. And because we are into election years in both Canada and the United States, no hard decisions are going to be made about facing up to economic reality.

Some of those concerns were behind Black Monday. They helped create a day of horror, a day that, within two months, wiped out the jobs of almost ten thousand people in the North American financial services sector. Ironically, many of those hit were the high-rolling yuppies. They had been on a high when the market surged. When it fell to the bears, they crashed and burned.

Combine over-consumption with over-indebtedness and you get collapse. That much is for sure—it's just the timing that's not. And it doesn't matter if we're talking about a person or a country or a continent. The risk is just as great—for those who can't see it coming. Like most of Canada's leading economists. Since the October stock market crash they have irresponsibly continued to insist that no problem exists. This is absolute garbage.

But the institutions these guys work for have a great interest in keeping the economy robust. And they know that at the heart of the matter is a confident consumer, somebody who's willing to dip further into savings, borrow more on credit cards, walk into a big mortgage and not be talked into cutting back.

A lot of what you've been told is simply a half-truth. Too many economists are focussing on the short-term,the next six or twelve months. They can't see past the November 1988 U.S. presidential elections. They say time and time again that there's no reason to expect more than a gentle and gradual and expected slowdown. But this is cold comfort to the people who've already been told to take a walk. Layoffs have hit, from the auto parts industry to the floor of the Toronto Stock Exchange. More are coming as corporations trim fat and position themselves for the inevitable downturn.

But, like I said, most economists are not telling you this. There is a fear that gloomy predictions about the economy will only make things worse. Maybe so. Black Monday showed what panic can do to wealth. But at the same time, Canadians have a right to be warned. If a few changes in your current spending/borrowing habits now can prevent family hardship later, then you should know what they are.

There is one voice currently saying some of the things that must be heard. It belongs to William Mackness, senior vice-president and chief economist of the Bank of Nova Scotia. It's rare now to have a bank economist take this role. As a journalist, I've learned it isn't even worth interviewing them any more. I'm tired of their Pollyanna pablum. But Mackness has the guts not just to pinpoint problems but to write publicly about them. Early in 1988 he published a pamphlet that should be required reading for the middle class.

On the surface, it looks like a yawner, with its less than gripping title of *The Great U.S. Trade and Payments Conundrum*. In it, though Mackness explains that the whole continent, and probably most of the globe, is at great risk because America has a cash flow problem. Short of war or depression, he points out, the States is going to fall another $100 billion in debt every year until well into the 1990s.

So what? Does the White House get repossessed?

In a way, maybe. A lot of the borrowed

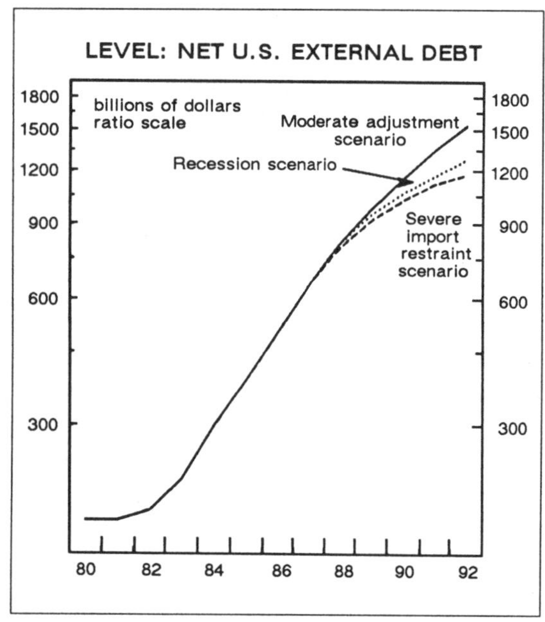

This chart shows what economist Mackness was talking about. The American debt to foreigners is huge and getting huger. Even a recession, or a strong bout of protectionism, isn't going to make the situation much worse. Good-bye America?

money comes from overseas, which means an increasing foreign debt for the U.S., a weakening dollar and, as a result, serious risks. The country can't be allowed to continue in that condition. This is the flower of capitalism, remember? If America fails, the system does, too. There *will* be a direct consequence, but right now we don't know what it will be.

It could take the form of high inflation, as the Federal Reserve—America's central bank—prints more money to afford these horrible debt payments. Rampant inflation is one of the greatest things the middle class must fear, because it destroys that part of your wealth that is paper: cash, investment certificates, savings bonds, term deposits and Treasury bills.

It could take the form of protectionism, as the U.S. tries to save jobs and stem the tide of imports swamping their country. The Canada–U.S. free trade treaty would either not be ratified or be simply bypassed. And that would mean bad news for Canada, which sends about three-quarters of all its exports south of the border. The job loss here would be awesome.

Or it could, Mackness points out, take the form of currency controls. Washington could impose limits on how much money left the country, in an attempt to stem the tide and slow national bankruptcy. Again, this would be a powerful signal to the rest of the world. This is a move you expect from a deadbeat Latin debtor nation,not from the U.S. of A..

But something has to give. Only a fool, or an economist with something to hide, could believe the current situation can continue. I've talked here about Canada's real debt problems, but they pale in global importance beside those the incoming American president must face.

In the early 1980s North Americans used

to shrug off the big deficits our governments ran up each year by saying we just owed that money to ourselves. For a while that was true—we did, in the form of government securities bought by institutions and savings bonds bought by us little people. But that's changed now. American indebtedness to foreigners was $200 billion five years ago. Today it's $650 billion. In five more years it will be over $1 trillion.

Canada is no better. Currently we owe foreigners more than $160 billion U.S. Paying just the interest on that costs us $20 billion a year. This is hard cash leaving the country. This is money we are generating through economic activity and then just giving away. At the same time we must borrow more money to meet the loan payments. It is a vicious, dangerous cycle. And it cannot go on forever.

On top of this, the Americans have a special problem with trade. Despite a weak dollar, they can't sell as much as they import. Every month last year they ran between $13 billion and $18 billion in the hole. Imports were $400 billion, or 65 percent, more than exports of $250 billion. So here's a country that borrows heavily from foreigners to finance government spending programs and at the same time sees its citizens buying imports and surrendering their earnings to foreign companies. In all, roughly $35 billion a month is bleeding away. And, clearly, that can't go on either.

Mackness has run over a few likely scenarios to see if they do much to help defuse this economic time bomb. He projected a rise in exports over imports, which may have started and has helped calm the stock market. He then determined what a wave of protectionism would do, closing American borders to imported products. Finally he looked at the effects of a very severe recession.

The results: "In each scenario, running from moderate adjustment to severe recession, the outcomes are depressingly similar. Reductions in the merchandise trade deficit are offset by a rising deficit on services transactions, which is mostly the result of rising interest payments on accumulated foreign debt.

"Our projections indicate that the U.S. current account deficit will remain above $100 billion [a year] on into the 1990s and that the level of foreign indebtedness will rise massively."

What that means is, there's no solution in sight. It means the country that was the world's banker and whose currency is the global standard is in vast danger. This is also the nation we've worked hard to hitch our star to. It is our chief market, and it dominates our economy. Its interest rates determine ours. We measure the value of our money against its currency.

So what America does to reverse its plight matters to us a hell of a lot. The next two years could be the most turbulent economic time in our history, more important than the economic expansion after World War Two, and more important than the decay of the Depression. The next guy in the Oval Office is going to have a profound effect on you and me and every other Canadian. Because we are so indebted ourselves, we've already surrendered our ability to set independent policy. Now we're just along for the ride.

The world today feels much different than it did just a year ago. It feels older, harder and more dangerous. I am not convinced Black Monday was an isolated event, or that we've seen the final results of that day. In fact, as I write this, Wall Street continues to stagger. The Dow Jones index jerks around by 100 points a day, something that would have seemed impossible a year ago.

But don't kid yourself—this stuff is not confined to the stock market. Instead what we have here is a warning signal. We're being told by these financial markets that the imbalances and excesses in the system just can't be ignored any longer. The world we live in is the most indebted in history. And it is also the most interconnected.

Things can go to hell one afternoon on Wall Street. Within hours that theme is picked up in Tokyo, then Sydney and Hong Kong. Markets in London and Paris awaken to fresh losses in Asia and open weak and nervous. As the afternoon arrives across the Atlantic, investors are looking to New York to see how trade will open there; looking for some rays of hope to end the down cycle. And so the circle completes itself every twenty-four hours. The potential to create a vortex of selling clearly exists. For the first time last October, we saw the viciousness it is capable of.

Computers, telecommunications links, satellites and integrated markets have set us up for a potential global collapse. More than ever, this is a time for strong leadership and the political will to take strong action. Deficits and debts have to be wiped out, or the panic that the markets are breeding could sweep into the rest of society. If it goes unchecked you will see everything from massive layoffs to the closing of banks. Last year almost 190 American banks failed. That toll will easily be surpassed this year. And yes, Canada will be hit, too.

Individual Canadians should realize that there are a lot of people working very hard to suppress the truth. Bank economists and some business leaders downplay the risk inherent in this economy. They don't tell you how close we are to recession or how the U.S. presidential elections in November will keep American policy paralyzed. It's true that this year we may encounter little more than an economic slowdown. But a serious reversal can't be avoided in 1989. It is not now a question of *whether* the economy will unravel—it's just *when*.

As always, this does not mean there won't be chances to make money. It just means we will all have to work harder at retaining our wealth, and we have to be cautious about some investments. Mutual funds and stocks are out. Cash is in. Gold is in. Silver is out. Treasury bills are in. Real estate is neutral.

In January 1987 I told my newsletter subscribers that federal tax reform would be "a con job" and offer us "some bitter surprises." I said that gold, then just three bucks over the $400 U.S./oz. mark, would climb by a hundred dollars. And I said that the stock markets were ignoring reality: "The stock market binge is taking place on a foundation of sand. Things are hot now, but they are also unsustainable. And when investors start running, some of them will get trampled."

Eight months later I made the warning louder. The U.S. economy is living on borrowed money and borrowed time, *The Survival Letter* said. And thirty-four days before the biggest collapse in history, I tried to tell people it was coming: "We feel the markets are at levels which are unsustainable. They may not totally collapse, but this is entirely possible.

"The red flag is out. Go back. Bail out. Take your profits while you can. This is not the place where safe money wants to be."

The advice was simple: Get out of stocks and mutual funds. Get into cash. And ditch all U.S. dollar investments.

Black Monday came, and went. But it was not alone. It was compounded immediatly afterward by a massive slide in the value of the American dollar—a crisis the central banks have been trying to deal with since.

There is, I believe, another shoe yet to drop. It may come while this book is being printed. Or it may wait until the summer of 1988. It may even wait until the early spring of 1989, when a new American president proves that real power has left the White House. This time it will become obvious to ordinary folks that what's going down on Bay Street and Wall Street is going to impact on their own lives. Those who can see it early will have the best chance of taking defensive action.

The chances I sensed were coming a year ago arrived, in spades:

- Gold did increase by $100 an ounce last year, closing through the $500 barrier one day last December.
- Interest rates bottomed out in March of 1987, then started a long and relentless climb. Only after stocks collapsed did frenzied governments work to shove them lower.
- Black Monday erased more wealth in a single day—about $2 trillion—than had ever been dreamed possible. It collapsed stock prices by almost a third, and was the worst decline ever. It made 1929 look like a picnic.
- Talk of recession became rampant. Suddenly the six-year-long business cycle was coming to a violent end. The layoffs began. At Chrysler and GM and Firestone. Then on Bay Street at Wood Gundy. And on Wall Street at Saloman Brothers, E. F. Hutton, Shearson Lehman, Merrill Lynch ... and the list goes on.
- In the last few months Canadians realized they have been on a spending spree financed not by cash flow but by dipping into savings. Our personal savings rate has fallen to a fourteen-year low. At the same time we have drastically increased our levels of personal debt. The annual reports of the big banks, released in the first few weeks of this year, gloated at the mushrooming size of their loan portfolios. At the Toronto Dominion alone, more than a thousand new mortgages were written, on average, every single week of the year.
- And while we were spending, inflation increased and wage gains did not. The average worker has been getting annual pay hikes of about 3 percent, while inflation is over 4 percent and rages at over 6 percent in hot spots like southern Ontario. That means our purchasing power is declining. The combination is eerie: low savings, high debt and slipping wages. Could we be more poorly prepared for an economic downturn? I really wonder.
- Tax reform was snuck in by a government that refused to make changes despite calls from members of Parliament, the Senate and thousands of Canadians. Now the capital gains tax holiday is gutted. Capital gains themselves will be taxed at a higher rate. All your savings are exposed to taxation. You are taxed on inflationary gains, dropping the real rate of return on invested money to just about zilch. The middle class is paying a disproportionate amount of tax. The self-employed are taxed more heavily. And government revenues will increase by billions this year and next. Can the economy survive this kind of robbery? Aren't the feds increasing the odds of a recession?
- Real estate roared into 1987 in a boom phase. Prices increased wildly as speculative excess gripped many markets

across the country. Then, in mid-April, the overheated market collapsed. Prices in places like Toronto fell 10 percent in just sixty days. The recovery has been spotty, and uncertainty has created real buying opportunities. And why not?

This country has a stable government, well-tuned industry, an educated workforce, great reserves of raw materials and unbridled access to the world's greatest consumer market. So despite the average house price of $200,000 in Toronto, there's a case for saying that land values in all of Canada are essentially undervalued. In Japanese yen, Hong Kong dollars or West German marks, Canadian real estate is absurdly cheap. Look for foreign investment to grow as the financial markets unwind and as investors search for a place where wealth can be safe. In the long-term, real estate will explode

Face it: no matter what the political stories are, or the disasters, no matter about the Iran–Iraq war coming to a bloody head this year, or serious troubles in Palestine, or anything else—there will be nothing more important this year than the economy.

As I said, the problems are much larger than most people realize, or than they are being told. And forget about that myth of social safety nets being in place to cushion the fall should the economy collapse. The reality is that the nets are not there. A widespread depression with 25 percent unemployment would quickly crush the system as it stands. Governments are technically bankrupt on this continent. All they've got is the ability to raise funds through borrowing.

In a depression, the tax take would be cut by at least a third while the demands placed on government would become much greater. The 1982 recession resulted in a $38 billion annual deficit. And despite almost six years of solid economic growth, we are still running annual shortfalls of close to $30 billion.

In many ways we are, as a country, far worse off than before this cycle started. Across Canada, there are huge differences in economic performance, which further cripples the federal government. The western markets never really came out of the 1982 recession, and prices remained depressed. So any prolonged downturn would be an awful experience. People lining up for unemployment benefits—after paying into the system all their working lives—could end up shocked at how little is left in the pot.

But this will not happen in 1988. Instead, we will start the slide. Growth will fall. Technically, we will enter a recession but the full effects will not be immediately felt. More likely, that will come in 1989.

With luck, interest rates should stay sane. And the Canadian dollar appears unlikely to head into any new crisis. This is because of the continuing poor health of the American buck whose only strength has come through a propping up by central banks. The alternative is for the U.S. to raise interest rates, but that would just bring the bad times sooner. The key is how Washington muddles through the rest of 1988. With the November election, there will be pressure to keep rates down and deflect the downturn until 1989.

In the meantime, some other things are becoming clear.

Canadians in general have a false and misguided sense of optimism. Polls show they did not take the stock crash seriously and are unaware of the country's foundation of debt. Such optimism, along with the blinding consumerism that drives the culture, leads them to continue depleting their savings exactly when that is the most dangerous thing possible. People are not conserving their cash. They do not realize that the best possible investment now is to reduce personal levels of debt. At greatest risk are over-mortgaged Canadians.

While real estate remains as an excellent long-term investment, this market is not without storm clouds. Single-family residential housing will emerge fairly intact. The commercial market will take a big dive in some regions—especially the west—as recession nears. And hardest hit will be the overextended condominium scene.

Thousands of these expensive units have been marketed and sold, particularly in the big cities. There are thousands more in the planning and approval stages. A shocking number have been purchased not as residences, but as investments. Investors think prices will endlessly increase, and many of them feel that when their unbuilt condos come on stream later this year or into 1989, they'll be able to flip them for big profits.

But the market is facing a glut, as it did about seven years ago. The condo marketers have been wildly successful in preselling, and a kind of buyer mania swept many people along. Once closing day rolls around, though, more than a few will regret they walked into the sales offices.

Probably the first sector of the economy to be hit in the coming, slower, months will be travel. Corporations will cut back on the amount of travelling they allow employees to do. Canadians, suddenly worried about layoffs and the interruption of their cash flow, will forgo expensive holidays to exotic destinations. Instead, they'll do a lot more day-tripping.

Over the next twenty months, increasing layoffs will deal consumer confidence a mortal blow. Sales of new homes will come to a virtual halt. Discretionary spending will slow. The home furnishings industry, a fast-grower since 1984, will suffer a major setback. Against this backdrop, people will be uncertain about the correct investment course.

Through it all, cash and liquid investments will be very important. Gold is likely to keep adding value, after a wave of weakness in the first few months of 1988. Once solidly through the $520 U.S./oz mark, it is poised to sail right through $600. And in an environment where interest rates remain very high relative to inflation, cash instruments like Treasury bills will perform well.

A good investment strategy: Pay down debt now. Maximize cash. Wait for the big downturn to materialize, then go bargain-hunting for quality real estate that overextended owners need to bail out of. Think like a vulture, and you'll do well.

Once layoffs cut into personal cash flow, there will be a mess of properties on the market, put there by people who can no longer service the mortgages. Just taking on those loans will be enough, in many cases, to secure title to the land. But to do that, you need cash.

So work hard and save hard. Stay lean; use common sense. Don't over-extend yourself. Don't take risks and don't believe everything you hear.

Things may get tough, but it's not over yet.

Chapter Two

Black Monday: The day the music died

I was rushed that morning. Every fourteen days I face another deadline in the production of two newsletters, one on real estate on the first of the month, the other on personal financial planning on the fifteenth.

This issue of *The Survival Letter* should have gone to the mailroom the Thursday before, but something inside was telling me to hold off. It was just as well. On Friday, October 16, 1987, the Dow Jones Industrial Average had plunged by over 100 points, one of the largest single-day declines in history. On Sunday the eighteenth I decided to revise my investment comments and to hold the newsletter back until noon the next day.

That Sunday afternoon I sat down and wrote this: "The American economy is very much at risk. Its currency is sliding. Its financial markets are under attack. It is a country which looks to others to finance its debt, and it owes more than anybody in the world. America has a bunch of losers running to be president, and it's being set up for a fall in the Persian Gulf."

That night in the gulf, U.S. Navy warships attacked and destroyed an Iranian oil platform which had been converted to a military command centre. After the bombardment, American forces boarded the platform and destroyed radar and communication gear.

In Tehran Iran's president called the move "a big mistake" and said his country would take "decisive retaliatory action."

In New York the market opened sharply lower in nervous trade. The same thing on Bay Street. In London, England, the *Financial Times* share index was taking a dive, largely in response to the Dow's disastrous Friday. By the end of the trading day there—midmorning in North America—the index was off 249.6 points. In a single session the market had lost almost 11 percent of its value. The fall was five times larger than anything ever experienced and almost 2 percent more than what Wall Street had suffered in all of the previous week.

In my office at *The Toronto Sun* I finished off the newsletter, called the printer to come and get it, then walked out to look at the Dow Jones news wire machine, which sits about ten feet away. It was 10:34 in the morning.

The American dollar had ended trading much lower in Europe. Weekend comments by U.S. Treasury Secretary James Baker, which hinted at conflicting monetary policy between the States and West Germany, had made things worse. The markets were down on the Yanks and looking for excuses to sell greenbacks. Here was one. Still, the buck registered at over 142 Japanese yen, far above the gut-busting 120-yen mark it would hit before all of these events were over.

News of the Iranian hit had boosted the dollar a touch, but the rally fizzled. Then trading opened on the New York Stock Exchange. The dollar plunged.

President Ronald Reagan had just issued a statement saying the oil platform attack had been a "prudent yet restrained response" to an Iranian attack on a Kuwaiti oil tanker. "The U.S. has no desire for a military confrontation with the government of Iran," he said. The Dow was down 104 points.

At 10:58 the Securities Exchange Commission, or SEC, the body that regulates the American financial markets, said it was "concerned" about the stock market plunge and was watching the situation. By 11:41 the Toronto Stock Exchange's 300 composite index, or TSE 300, was off by 213 points. Declining issues beat advances by a seven-to-one ratio.

The only bright spot was with gold shares; and the gold mining index was up 4 percent. In London the afternoon gold price had just been fixed: $481 U.S. an ounce, up $2 from the morning and $16 ahead of where it had closed Friday afternoon. A lot of worried money was fleeing the stock market, looking for safety.

By noon the tape that records stock transactions in Toronto was running an hour late so, traders didn't know what kind of a market they were selling into. The TSE 300 was down 194 points. By one o'clock, the index had fallen another 20 points, and now even gold shares were being hit. With three hours of trading left before the closing bell, a record had already been set in New York, with 338.5 million shares changing hands. The New York trading tape was running eighty-five minutes late. The Dow was down 171 points. Ten minutes later came the first indication that the SEC might, for the first time in history, close down the stock exchange.

The thought of doing this in a market-driven, free-enterprise capitalist nation is overwhelming. In fact, only the U.S. president has the direct authority to do such a thing. By 1:30 SEC chairman David Ruder had not yet called Reagan. That would come later. But in Washington Ruder told reporters, "There is some point, and I don't know what that point is, that I would be interested in talking to the New York Stock Exchange about a temporary, very temporary, halt in trading." This news further electrified the market. Systematic selling became panic unloading.

The Dow was down 189 points when I ripped the latest copy off the wire, had it photographed, cut it into my newsletter and gave it to the waiting courier. Within a few dozen hours several thousand subscribers would get this analysis of a hopelessly complex event, the depths of which nobody could yet plumb. In my stomach I felt there was more to come—much more. The day was turning into one of horrified fascination. It was like watching an execution. Witnesses say they couldn't bear to watch. And they couldn't bear not to watch. History was visiting this day, Monday, October 19, 1987.

By now declining stocks were beating advancing ones by an unbelievable ratio of twenty-five to one. The tape was running eighty minutes late. A Merrill Lynch trader told Dow Jones that what was happening was an "emotional purging sequence." He could not have been more correct.

At two o'clock the TSE 300 was off 237.54 points. In New York and Chicago the futures markets were being nuked. Selling had reached panic proportions. In the House of Commons, Finance Minister Mike Wilson was asked what he was going to do about the stock crisis. Nothing, he said. Wilson said he had confidence in the economy and saw no need for "precipitate action." He said: "Let's wait and see what happens."

Ten minutes later Ronald Reagan went public, trying to reassure the market that a falling dollar, troubles with Iran, rising interest rates, a horrible trade deficit, overextended financial markets and oceans of government red ink were no cause for alarm. The Gipper worked hard at being positive and optimistic. The economic expansion had been long and good, he said. Unemployment was at a decade-long low. Personal and family incomes had been rising, and leading economic indicators were "sending a message: Steady as she goes."

And go she did. Within a few minutes the Dow was down by 264 points. Massive losses were experienced as widespread panic gripped Wall Street. At this point the Dow was off 11.75 percent on the day. Not since October 28, 1929 had the Dow ever suffered a one-day setback of more than 12 percent. But maybe this would be the day. And that's when the talk of a new Depression started.

By three o'clock Doug Creighton, chairman of the *Toronto Sun*, said he wanted an eight-page section published on the crash, and a hasty meeting of reporters, editors and columnists took place in my office. We sketched out plans for coverage, and I assigned stories to different people. Swing editor Kay Corbett got the job of laying out a page with pictures of riots, food lines and shanty towns in Toronto during the 1930s. The atmosphere was getting tense.

Within twenty minutes the Dow was down 342 points. By now the market had declined 15 percent, and over 500 million shares had changed hands. The tape was two hours slow. It took fourteen more minutes for another 25 million shares to trade and for the index to drop 40 points. And then, things went into freefall.

In the final hour there was simply no stopping events. Now decliners were beating advancers by forty to one. The Dow dropped another 120 points, and at the closing bell the market had been decimated by a 508-point crash. This represented a 22.62 percent decline and was, as a NYSE official put it, a "financial meltdown." The entire year's gains had been erased in just seven and a half hours. Over 600 shares traded. Brokerages stayed open most of the night trying to process the mountains of sell orders.

When the analysis started, the common view emerged that this day marked the end of the five-year-long bull market, that investors had been spooked by the falling dollar, rising interest and most of all by a frightening lack of confidence in Ronald Reagan's ability to deal with a decaying economy.

This was the day the American empire ended.

The selling had come from individuals and institutions, from foreigners and Americans. Mutual funds were unloading, and leveraged investors were plagued with margin calls—made by brokers who were themselves facing a financial abyss. And the rumors started. E. F. Hutton was about to go down. Company executive Edward Lill categorically denied the whispers. "Our trading floors are holding up reasonably well," he said. "Our losses are not that great." He was lying. Hutton was bleeding internally and would soon disappear within the womb of Shearson Lehman. The layoffs would be ghastly. "I had to back away from the use of the word financial 'panic,' " one investment strategist said. "But I'm using that reluctantly. This has got to be financial panic worldwide."

Sadly, it was far more than that. This day signalled the end of an entire economic order.

I got home late that night, watched the fire and drank scotch. When I went to bed the Tokyo market was just opening. Early trading in Japan, Hong Kong and Singapore would be brutal, and events this morning on the European money markets would be crucially important. Black Monday was over, but the story was just beginning. I set my radio alarm to hear the first dispatches from the Orient.

It wasn't the stock market crash of 1929 that caused the real damage. It was the consequences of that crash, which didn't hit until the next year. Fifty-eight years later, as bad as Black Monday was, it was the next day, Tuesday, October 20, that almost destroyed the financial system of the Western world.

The morning news from Asian markets was horrible. Tokyo, Singapore, Sydney and Hong Kong were in a rout. Officials soon decided to close the Hong Kong market, a move that proved to be a big mistake. The day it reopened, it lost almost half its value.

I drove to Toronto a half-hour before the markets opened. There was nothing but talk of "the crash of '87" on the radio. There were stock market jokes already. (What do you call a yuppie stockbroker? "Waiter!") There was also a lot of heavy talk about what might happen on this crucial day. Overnight some securities firms on Wall Street were stunned when they had called banks looking for loans and were refused.

Bankers Trust was telling clients it wouldn't extend credit that wasn't fully secured by assets. Big Japanese banks threatened to entirely stop lending. Suddenly a stock market crisis threatened to turn into something far worse—a credit crisis. If the flow of money stopped, then the big investment houses would start to topple. Investment banking companies would collapse. It would be a rerun of the days leading up to the Great Depression.

The American central bank—the Federal Reserve, or Fed—took a leadership role in the absence of any political direction from Washington. President Reagan had choked the day before. The country's system was coming unravelled, and all the White House could say was that it was "concerned."

The crisis was acute enough that all the rules had to change. Sensing imminent disaster, the Fed put out a one-line statement that was a shocking departure from the past. It was ready, it said, "to serve as a source of liquidity to support the economic and financial system."

After months of tightening up the money supply, hiking interest rates and worrying about inflation, the Fed pulled a complete about-face. Within minutes it started flooding the system with money. It bought up government securities and acted to drive interest rates down. Ottawa mirrored the move, but much more quietly. The Bank of Canada told the country's big banks that it would make available to them all the money they needed. And two days later the bank dropped its key interest rate by well over 1 percent, the biggest single-day drop in history.

Fed officials got on the phone and warned America's bankers they were in deep trouble if they didn't continue normal lending practices. But on the New York Stock Exchange things were far from normal.

There were simply no buyers, and so trading was close to impossible. Even blue chip stocks took an hour or more to open, but when they did, prices were higher. The Dow's opening posted an amazing 200-point gain. That didn't last long, though. Initial optimism turned to grinding despair as big investment firms seized the opportunity to unload, immediately driving prices lower. Stock exchange officials now openly worried that global financial panic would destroy the market. And they were close to the truth.

One by one, trading in major stocks broke down. Regulators were horrified. By noon stock chairman John Phelan was calling a meeting to decide whether the exchange should close down to stem the panic. The market was now down 100 points. Losses had the potential to at least double before the day ended. Rumors were again swirling that major companies were about to fall. Some of the world's largest investment firms were secretly calling the Securities Exchange Commission, begging them to close the market.

But in the end Phelan decided against it. Shutting up, he said, would be a bad signal, a psychological blow against America that would be felt around the world. Besides, after closing, how could thousands of stocks be reopened? Where would the buyers come from? "If we close it," Phelan said grimly, "we would never open it."

Shortly before noon I arrived at the midtown studios of CHUM-FM, the most listened-to radio station in the country. Every Tuesday I give a commentary on business and economics and money in general with veteran broadcaster Larry Wilson. This day neither one of us smiled much. The world was falling apart. The Dow and the TSE 300 were bleeding badly. Investor confidence was in shreds. Confusion and anxiety and thoughts of 1929 were in everybody's head.

Before turning on his mike, Wilson put a piece of paper on the cloth-covered table of the broadcast booth. It was a memo from company president Allan Slaight. There had to be some good news somewhere in what was happening, Slaight had told his newsmen. Find it.

Actually, it was starting to happen. While Wilson and I tried to be brave about events, saying the market had been overvalued and ripe for a correction and things may appear worse than they were, a few big traders on Wall Street were getting smart. A dramatic rally was staged on the Major Market Index, a collection of twenty blue chip stocks intended to mirror activity on the Dow. Trading was so light that a few bold moves by a very few dealers sent this index spiralling higher. It was the first, faint bullish move that the market had been looking for, and as a result of it, some buyers started to materialize.

Then a number of large companies announced they were going to start buying back their own stock. This came after major investment firms had urged hundreds of corporate clients to make exactly these kinds of announcements. Both moves—buying Major Market futures contracts and the buy-back plans—were clearly engineered by a handful of people who stepped into a crisis. Combined with the Fed's move to shower everyone with money, the day was saved. By closing, the Dow was up 102.27 points, with over 608 million shares changing hands. On Wednesday the rally continued, and the gain was over 186 points. Over the next few weeks, there were more substantial gains and several bad losses. Market trading patterns had been shattered. The course of financial—maybe economic—history had been changed.

The system survived Tuesday, but just barely. It took luck, extraordinary moves and unprecedented intervention. Most of those who engineered the day's salvation ended it close to disbelief.

That morning the *Wall Street Journal* had opened its coverage with one simple line: "The stock market crashed yesterday." Over two hundred reporters and editors had covered the story. For the first time ever the *Journal* used a two-column headline. A front-page article asked: If this was worse than 1929, "can it happen again?"

The theme was to be with us for months. The disturbing realization was that this crash, this meltdown of the financial system, had happened at a time when there was no real crisis. There was no Vietnam war on. No Chernobyl. No assassination attempt on the American president. No crop failures. It had come, rather, as a response to slightly higher interest rates, a dirty little skirmish in the Persian Gulf, a declining currency and trade imbalances. Worrisome, but hardly apocalyptic.

Here was a society of immense wealth. Here was a middle class aspiring to BMWS. Here was a city—New York—where Wall Street kids in their twenties were taking home six-figure paycheques and commit-

THE WALL STREET JOURNAL.

© 1987 Dow Jones & Company, Inc. All Rights Reserved.

TUESDAY, OCTOBER 20, 1987 — SHARON, PENNSYLVANIA — 50 CENTS

Market Fallout

The Crash of '87

Stocks Plunge 508.32 Amid Panicky Selling

Percentage Decline Is Far Steeper Than '29; Precious Metals Gain

YORK – The stock market ... yesterday.

... Dow Jones Industrial Average ... an astonishing 508.32 points, or ...%, to 1738.42. The drop far exceeded ... 12.8% decline on the notorious day of ... Oct. 28, 1929, which is generally considered the start of the Great Depression.

Panic-driven trading on the New York Stock Exchange reached 604,801,000 shares, nearly double the prior record volume of 338.5 million shares set last Friday, when the Dow plunged a then-record 108.35 points.

This article was prepared by Wall Street Journal staff reporters Tim Metz, Alan Murray, Thomas E. Ricks and Beatrice E. Garcia.

Commodities prices also plunged, except for precious metals and especially gold, which surged $10.10 an ounce to $481.70, a 4½-year high. The bond market, a refuge for much of the capital being wrenched out of the stock market, recovered from steep early losses to end the day higher.

Final Slide

The industrial average tumbled the last 130 points in the final 30 minutes of the session. The decline yesterday and last week totaled 743.79 points, or 30%. By way of comparison, the total drop on Oct. 28 and Oct. 29, 1929 was 71.15 points, or 23.6%.

With yesterday's drop, the industrial ...

HOW TO RENT A furnished office in Canada For a day, a week, a month or a year. DRAKE INTERNATIONAL BUSINESS CENTRES

The Globe and Mail

CANADA'S NATIONAL NEWSPAPER

144th YEAR, NO. 43,017 • METRO • TUESDAY, OCTOBER 20, 1987

Sunrise 7:39 Sunset 6:28 Showers High near 11

CANADA LIFE The Canada Life Assurance Company

Panic sweeps financial markets smashing records of 1929 crash

BY GAIL LEM
The Globe and Mail

Share prices crumbled on stock exchanges around the world yesterday as a classic financial panic swept the equity markets.

The decline was of epic proportions. Fortunes were lost in a matter of hours as the New York Stock Exchange suffered a gut-wrenching collapse — far worse than that recorded during the massive stock market crash of 1929 that ushered in the Great Depression.

The Dow Jones industrial average, the most widely watched measure of share values on Wall Street, buckled by 508.32 points or 22.62 per cent. It closed at 1,738.41.

The sudden financial meltdown has resurrected fears that the global economy is about to slide into a recession. It more than wiped out the gains made on the NYSE since the beginning of the year, bringing the Dow barometer — which includes the world's best blue-chip stocks and is sometimes said to be a monitor of the fiscal heartbeat of the United States — back to where it stood on April 7, 1986.

In percentage terms, it was a disaster — almost double the mark of 12.9 per cent recorded on Oct. 28, 1929. In point terms, it easily eclipsed last Friday's record plunge of 108.35 points — itself a wipeout that just two weeks ago was considered unthinkable.

But politicians in Ottawa and Washington were sanguine, pointing out that the price drops in the market were out of step with advances in the economy.

The October massacre left no major financial market on the globe untouched. The value of shares listed on the Toronto Stock Exchange

STOCK — Page A2

Spectators in the ... Toronto Stock Ex...

The plunge at a glance

...f '29? ...n in '87 ...xpected

...NETH H. BACON
THE WALL STREET JOURNAL

This was the first edition in the history of the Wall Street Journal *that used a two-column headline on its front page. Nothing before had merited more than one column. The* Globe's *front page headlines were in my view an error in judgment. The situation was so volatile on the morning following the crash that comparisons with 1929 were completely inappropriate. In many ways, it turned out that Tuesday was worse than Black Monday. The system came a lot closer to meltdown.*

ting to buy million-dollar condos.

Materialism had become an end of its own. Here was a society possessed by the achievement of financial goals.

Gone from this generation was any idealism or genuine concern with things like honesty. When David Levine, Ivan Boesky and others were busted for making millions trading on inside stock information, they were more folk heroes than bandits. Those who looked on in shock also looked on in fascination. When Bernard Goetz mowed down a bunch of black kids on a subway car, he was mobbed by admirers. When *Wall Street Journal* columnist R. Foster Winans was found to have leaked advance information so that others could trade on it, he met a tidal wave of sympathy, and his book on the subject became a bestseller.

One of television's most popular shows, "L.A. Law," featured a bunch of overpaid young lawyers who competed for corporate favors and compensation, drove expensive foreign cars and enjoyed sexual liaisons with friends and aquaintances. Yet were they *happy*?

Some say October 19 was the culmination of a series of events that started with the insider trading scandals and went on to include the revelation that Gary Hart was shacking up with actress Donna Rice. Hart was unquestionably a yuppie hero—the square-jawed neo-liberal who didn't talk about deficit financing and wore expensively tooled cowboy boots. He did in life what the lawyers did on T.V., but it was unacceptable behavior for a public figure. The leading yuppies of the day were showing that they could not cap the consumerism, materialism and egotism in their own lives. If it felt good, it *was* good. Disparities in wealth were justified. The economic order was cashing in its conscience. It used to be that Volvos were advertised as a good investment because they were safe and lasted a long time. Now they were portrayed as luxury sedans that physically rewarded the person who drove them.

And here was Ivan Boesky, a man of untold wealth. He was using illegally obtained information to add millions more to the millions he already found it impossible to spend. Worse, it did not begin or end with him. Dozens of others were involved, and for several weeks The Street lived in fear after it was revealed that Boesky had cheated on yuppiedom by wearing a wire for the feds during the last of his deals. This was the zenith of greed, accompanied by the man's outlandish consumption. Yet, he had been a pillar of the community, a big patron of the arts.

Finally there was Col. Oliver North, a cowboy superpatriot out of control in the White House basement. North was a yuppie in uniform, driving on with the characteristic blinkers of ego firmly in place. Here was the man who engineered arms sales to Iran, the nation of zealots that had shamed the U.S. during the hostage-taking of 1979. He had bypassed his superiors and short-circuited the political system. His actions were typical in their motivation: mindless ambition; disregard for traditional moral codes; slavish adherence to self-inspired dogma. The medals on the man's chest were the military equivalent of the Rolex watch, the seven-series BMW and the unlivably big house that his civilian counterparts sought. Ollie North, his shredder, and his yuppie/beauty secretary Fawn Hall stood together as the latest symbols of excess.

Fast food. Fast cars. Fast money. Fast heroes. Things sure were different from the generation that had come before, the one whose work ethic and personal view of the world had been shaped first by Depression and then by war.

In almost every way, Black Monday was as overdue as it was inevitable. The yuppies learned something that day: there are cycles. For my generation, one had just ended.

But why didn't we see it coming? Probably because we didn't want to.

God knows there were enough warning signs; enough deteriorating conditions; and, especially, enough departures from the past, with the lessons parents learned in the Depression giving way to the lifestyle goals of their kids. There was also a special arrogance here, a feeling of generational invincibility. It was the three-pack-a-day man believing he was immune to lung cancer. It was the gambler on a streak, suddenly believing it was him, not his luck. It was time to fly in the face of history, to forget that the eighties were mirroring the twenties. It was the arrogance to think that, for some reason, it was okay this time to dip into the cookie jar. Up to your damn elbows. This was the feeling in the days of frozen yogurt, compact discs and suspenders.

On August 25 the Dow topped out at 2722.42, up an incredible 800 points in just ten months. The generational arrogance had found expression in the very way the markets did business. First there was speculative excess and a belief I heard time and time again that the bull market was intact and would rise virtually forever. In the summer of 1987 it was almost impossible to find anyone advising clients to take profits. Among the few who did were broker Tony Reid, in the newspaper column he writes for me, and Toronto forecaster Ian McAvity. Mostly, caution was being sacrificed on the greasy altar of greed. Why should anyone cash out now and miss the gains yet to come?

Stock prices climbed higher and higher. And as they did The Street dreamed up the justification for it all. It was a big influx of Japanese money (when, it fact, investment levels were falling off). It was caused by a shortgage of "quality" shares, and so demand was simply pushing values higher—completely normal stuff. Or maybe it was just a robust economy, complete with lower inflation, lower unemployment and lower business morals.

Market heights more or less corresponded with frenzied takeover, acquisition and leveraged buy-out activity in corporate America. Suddenly multibillion-dollar deals were making headlines every week. Suddenly the market came to believe that anything could happen, that it was probably impossible to pay too much for anything and that rumors were facts.

The height of absurdity came in the third week of June. In Cincinnati somebody named David Herrlinger, an investment advisor nobody had ever heard of, announced a $6.8-billion offer to purchase Dayton Hudson Corporation. Herrlinger gave an interview on his front lawn and, when asked if this was a hoax, said it was "no more a hoax than anything else." Instead of realizing the wisdom this fool spoke, the market took it seriously. The value of the retailer's stock soared, trading was intense, and over five million shares changed hands. David Herrlinger ended up in hospital for psychiatric observation.

This was also the time when corporate raiders were making their names and their fortunes. Raiders like Carl Icahn would buy enough stock in a company to horrify the board of directors. They'd quickly make a deal with him to buy back the shares at outrageously inflated prices, using shareholders' money. The price of the stock would rise on the market, and the raider would walk away with extra millions—all for not doing something he'd threatened. These people, in turn, had their extravagant lifestyles catalogued in the pages of *Fortune* magazine or the *New York Times*. We had new role models. We were being asked to admire these people, for their wealth and nothing more.

At the same time there was a big drop in the quality of investments. Billions worth of buy-outs and takeovers were financed with junk bonds, high-yield, high-risk securities backed only by the value of the companies who were issuing them. It even came to the point where non-performing Third World loans were being bundled into junk bonds and peddled to investors. Suddenly a way had been found to recycle debt, to raise more money on old loans. It tied in beautifully with a market that encouraged speculating against even itself, using stock index options available on margin.

Meanwhile there were the arbitrage traders, guys like Ivan Boesky. They made their money on speculation, on the possibility of takeover or buy-out announcements (or rumors) that made stock prices jump. They would take huge risks, and reap huge returns if the gamble was right. In a business like this, insider trading information was a solid and productive asset.

Suddenly gone were the old rules of investing—looking at the corporations whose shares you were buying, doing a technical analysis of the stock and staying away from shares that were overvalued. Now nothing was too expensive, because it would only go higher. The stock market came to symbolize too much. It was too closely allied with the identity of a whole class of people. Investment levels in stock-based mutual funds had exploded. The Investment Funds Institute of Canada had never recorded numbers like that before. Middle-income Canadians in early 1987 flocked to put their retirement dollars into funds that boldly claimed to make them 15 percent or better. Nowhere, however, were the risks spelled out. Worrying about risk was for wimps. Calling your broker was for achievers. For the first time in Canadian history, several large investment houses ran prime-time television commercials.

Black Monday came as a genuine shock to most market players. The speed and severity of the decline stunned them. In the days immediately after there was a denial factor. Brokers and traders and errand boys had come to think they were securely employed. Consumers were sure this "stock market thing" would not spill over into the real economy.

During the last two weeks of October, retail sales actually increased in Canada and the U.S. Car sales were healthy. Jaguar of Canada reported one of its best sales periods ever. Honda's recently launched luxury Acura line did big numbers. Real estate in Toronto made a nice late-autumn comeback.

On Bay Street and Wall Street, however, it did not take long for the awesomeness of events to start sinking in. While credit card–toting consumers could deny reality and delay payments, corporations caught in the market crossfire could not. And when the markets did not bounce blithely back to match the pre-crash highs, when it was obvious that the bull was dead, then the hurt started.

Six months before Black Monday it had been predicted that a major correction in the markets would lead to recession and substantial layoffs, which would first hit the financial services sector. And they did. As a direct result of the crash, E. F. Hutton was forced to merge with Shearson Lehman Holdings, with the eventual loss of as many as 6000 jobs on Wall Street. In the sixty days following October19 about 4000 jobs had already disappeared, including 800 at Salomon Brothers, 1000 at Kidder Peabody, 400 at Goldman Sachs and 100 at junk bond specialist Drexel Burnham. Giant Citicorp decided to trim its ranks by 5000, with 1000 of those going from its New York branches.

In Canada the fallout came later. Troubled Wood Gundy cut 150 people loose. Merrill Lynch Canada laid off another 180, and in January cuts started at the Toronto Stock Exchange itself. In Vancouver, Canadian Equity Planners, a financial planning firm, closed its doors, putting 250 out of work. Here was a company that had declared a $200,000 profit in the year ending July 31. But after Black Monday it was all over. Sales volumes had been chopped by 50 percent.

"I'm being very upfront about this," company president Wayne Holmgren told reporters. "I'm seeing that if an industry at large is in a certain amount of difficulty and we're losing money and there's no quick fix ... then we're only fooling ourselves by buying a little time. If you go that route, you lose a lot of money."

In a way, this is a problem we all face. What does a middle class Canadian do? Do we ignore Black Monday and say it's a problem for the boys at Merrill Lynch or E. F. Hutton? Or do we take it as a warning cry, a tremor of substantive change?

On the afternoon of October 19 I was convinced that what we were seeing was the breaking up of an expansionary cycle that had run amok. Economics had been twisted by socials. Here was prosperity strangely crafted from debt. Here was wealth without the production of goods. Business was not a function of society—society had become business. Since that day nothing has come along to change my mind. I see an old order struggling to keep what's left of the system intact—by changing some rules, saying reassuring things, appointing boards of inquiry—but the battle has already been lost. We will eventually return to more traditional values, which, ironically, will come through a new wave of liberal thinking.

But with that change there's going to be more grief, some brushes with panic and a lot of soul-searching. The ways we've learned to use money in the 1980s will have to change. So will our thoughts on debt, leveraging and repayment. Our country will be doomed unless the political will emerges to pull it back from the brink of financial enslavement. When the rescue comes, it's going to call for both sacrifice and understanding. Neither, I'm afraid, are part of the yuppie view of things. But in the world coming, gratification for the hell of it will be looked at a bit like smoking is today.

How fast this world changes into the next one is still an open question. Our economy is now 55 percent-driven by consumer spending. If consumers get too shocked too fast, they could pull back and turn a business slowdown into economic armageddon. As a journalist, I was intensely aware that Black Monday, for a few dozen hours, had the potential to do that.

In the meeting in my *Toronto Sun* office that was called to plan our coverage of the day, I said we could possibly become as much a part of the problem as any speculator on Bay Street moving paper to save his financial butt. The stories we wrote were sensational and exhaustive, yes, but they were consciously written not to be fearmongering. I had reservations about harking back to the city's Depression past, but events of the day called out for exactly that.

The next day Slaight's memo at CHUM-FM wasn't being taken lightly. But neither would any seasoned newsman feel constrained to understate the facts. As Larry Wilson and I went on the air that day, both of us were more deeply shaken than we let on. The audience for this broadcast is huge; the daily readership of my newspaper column is roughly 200,000. There is clearly a responsibility there not to unduly sway public opinion. And now, months after the event, I can say what I am saying. That day changed our society. It had the potential to collapse it into a high-tech dark ages. We were that close.

Two days later I was on Global Television's noon newscast. That day the TSE 300 would fall another 100 points. I stressed that the best possible course was for people to take all their money and throw it in the current issue of Canada Savings Bonds. The bond rate had been set at a pre-crash level of 9 percent. That reflected conditions then—interest rates were on the rise and investors thought they could do a lot better with a high-flying mutual fund. Before Black Monday and the subsequent huge drop in interest rates, 9 percent had looked kind of mediocre.

But after October 19 it was a small-time investor's dream. Eventually almost $15 billion worth of bonds were doled out by Ottawa, massively higher than the usual amount. This was, I told viewers, no time for anything other than secure, no-surprises, riskless and calculated investments. And, more than ever, it was critically important to save.

I was not yet telling people not to spend. That came about four weeks later, when I did one of my regular commentaries for "Money$Worth", a popular personal financial planning show carried by TV Ontario. For the first time I made a simple point: nothing is more important in the coming months than to stop spending, assess your situation, take cash and pay down debt. I told viewers to watch the show, turn off the television, go to the kitchen table and decide on a plan of survival. Then they should go to the bank and make repayment plans while they still had the option.

It was not the show's usual fare, and I think it upset some of the people involved. Going on network television and telling people to turn of the T.V., I guess, is not usually done. But they didn't stop me from saying it.

A couple of weeks later, Bruce Rogers, one of the show's two hosts gave me a cartoon he'd drawn. It was me, flying over the city on a carpet, finger in the air, saying, "Now I don't want to alarm you, but ..."

The times, they were changing.

Canadians are different from Americans. We take fewer risks, expect more from government and are suspicious of achievers. It's no surprise that twice as many Americans, as a percentage of the population, are stock market investors, or that homelessness is a vastly greater problem there. Americans are more willing to tolerate a society that endures low points as long as it regains the highs. They define democracy as the ability to fail. Without that, there would be no opportunity to succeed.

I think Canadians are slower to accept that the economy is in trouble. We take events less seriously. We feel falsely insulated. Perhaps we should use Americans as early-warning systems.

Just over three months after Black Monday, Decision Research, a Kentucky-based company, conducted 3500 interviews in seven surveys. The results were fascinating, and eloquent.

"A damoclean sword is hanging over the U.S. economy," the report read, "held by the gossamer thread of consumer confidence." The surveys found that American opinions about what the future held fluctuated wildly. There were significant swings in sentiment from one day to the next—more evidence that the values and beliefs of the previous decade were breaking down. While 10 percent said the October crash had caused them to cut back on purchases or to sell off stock holdings, another 40 percent said that only if the economy continued to be uncertain would they alter the way they managed their family finances. For them, Black Monday was not as much an event as it was a symbol of "uncertainty and instability in the economy."

Almost half said they'd probably cancel vacation plans or put off a major purchase unless the economy stabilized. The response of those over sixty years of age deserves special attention: they were the most convinced that the U.S. was headed for another Depression. "It's a bit troublesome," one researcher said, "since these are the people who saw the approach of the Great Depression." You bet it is.

Also early in 1988 came the revelation that many of those corporate stock buyback plans that helped stave off disaster on Tuesday, October 20 had been nothing more than stunts. Although almost a thousand corporations had announced buybacks worth $38 billion U.S., only a tiny fraction had actually come through. And a lot of corporate managers admitted that they'd made those announcements just to bolster confidence, to send a signal out to little investors, to trick them.

This is how Shearson Lehman vice-president Peter DaPuzzo put it to the *New York Times*: "We called and cried 'Help.' We said: 'You needed Wall Street three years ago when you issued stock. Now Wall Street needs you.' Things were irrational and people thought the world was coming to an end. Many, many times there was pleading from an emotional point of view."

Brokers had pleaded with corporate clients to make confidence-bolstering buyback announcements. Months later it was clear there had never been any commitment to go through with it, even though not doing so was against U.S. securities laws. The SEC has been investigating, but it's also made it clear that no charges are likely to be laid. There is still that gossamer thread to worry about ...

And exactly how thick is it? The reality is that, months after the big event, almost nothing has changed. "The crash was like a giant tapping on the shoulder," American billionaire Ross Perot said. "But what have we done about the deficit? Nothing. What have we done about Third World loans? Nothing. What have we we done about our savings and loan system? Nothing. We had this big shock. Everybody was frightened. But now we're just kind of bumbling along."

As nervous as the average guy might be on some days, the appreciation of what Black Monday meant just isn't there yet. This tremendously important and moving signal of change was treated more as a media event than anything else. It will take another crash, or a sustained bear market, to underscore the significance of what is going on. Some analysts have suggested that when most people are relatively bouyant about the future, things will just end up worse. After all, it's one thing to expect problems and then cope with them. It's entirely another to be stunned with unexpected bad news.

In a market-driven capitalist society, what Wall Street does is vitally important. There are no barometers of society more sensitive. After Black Monday there was tremendous concern about the American budget deficit, so Congress and the White House hammered out a two-year reduction package. The market responded by going down. Then there were huge worries about the American trade deficit, which hit an astounding $17 billion in October. But when the figure dropped to just over $13 billion the next month—as announced in December—the market shrugged it off in two days. Analysts began speculating that the number wasn't correct. And all eyes looked forward to the next trade figure announcement.

All this points out that the numbers don't matter much. More important is the belief that the world's greatest country is in serious condition. Its moral decline has been translated into a void of leadership. In his final months in office, Ronald Reagan was a discredited liability. His administration had been rattled by the Iran-Contra affair, by scandals involving cabinet members and by his inability to inspire public confidence. The American space program was in tatters. In one year the U.S.S.R. launced ninety-nine satellites and set a record for the longest manned space flight, aboard their orbiting space station. During the same time NASA successfully launched only six satellites, and not a single American went into space.

The space shuttle remained on the ground. U.S. technology failed to perfect a booster rocket flawless enough to send it into orbit. This was the same year that Mikhail Gorbachev became "Gorby" to the American people; that he published a bestselling book; and that his American publisher placed newspaper ads nationwide proclaiming him "statesman of the year."

All of this was clearly connected, by more gossamer threads. The American empire is collapsing in on itself, and the last to know will be those at the centre. The process stands to be accelerated over the coming months. The man who becomes president will have the greatest reconstruction job on his hands since Franklin Roosevelt—and yet there is nobody of F.D.R.'s stature even running for the job. As Canadians, who see America as our largest and most important market, we have much to fear. Black Monday was simply the loudest, sharpest and most visible sign of a process that is now probably irreversible. The United States is in deep trouble.

Accelerating the collapse is the massive division of global wealth. Money has been flowing in a torrent out of North America to Europe and the Far East. The Organization for Economic Co-operation and Development has warned that without concerted international change, we are headed for a powerful recession. America must cut deeply into its budget deficits. West Germany has to stimulate its economy and create more demand for American goods. Japan has to restructure its economy and open its doors to foreign imports.

So far these kinds of changes have not been made. And until they are, a second market crisis is a real possibility. When it comes, the little guys—the middle-class people who thought this was Wall Street's problem—will suddenly realize it is much later in the day then they thought. In the final months of Reagan's eight-year administration, it has become clear that Reaganomics was really voodoo economics. Here was a man who had given the U.S.

citizen lower taxes while he drastically increased federal spending. Americans had been lulled into a sense of security by the great communicator while their country was letting foreigners come to hold the national mortgage. Suddenly executives from the Bank of America were over in Tokyo, looking for help in bailing out the institution. Suddenly all of the world's top banks were Japanese, and General Motors was importing cars from Mexico.

As 1987 ended, this is how editors of the *Wall Street Journal* ranked the year's top ten stories:

1) Black Monday
2) Insider trading scandals
3) The widening U.S. trade deficit
4) The decline of the U.S. dollar
5) Texaco and Pennzoil suing each other
6) The Third World debt
7) Paul Volcker quits the Fed; Alan Greenspan takes over
8) Wall Street firms consolidate
9) Airline safety deteriorates
10) Foreigners purchase U.S. assets.

Most of those stories are just variations on one theme. Together they show that the decline of the American empire has accelerated dramatically. If the list had been compiled by a non-business newspaper, it probably would have contained things like the defrocking of Gary Hart, the Jim and Tammy Bakker religious sex scandal, the Iran-Contra affair, and the AIDS crisis. It's pretty depressing stuff.

So, what comes next?

Virtually anything, it seems. There is clearly going to be no quick answer to the deficit problems faced by Canada and the U.S. Politicians on both sides of the border continue to pretend that their countries are not falling under the financial control of other nations. They continue to surrender sovereignty just so North Americans can live a lifestyle that they can't afford.

Neither Canada nor the U.S. has the ability to set its own interest rates. The States has to act to protect its dollar. We are forced to keep our rates higher than those to the south so we can attract the foreign investment we need to survive.

In an environment like this, individual Canadians must first make themselves aware of the threats, and then set out on a course of action. One of the best plans is to do exactly the opposite of what the government is doing. If tough times are coming, you need to be ready for them. If our largest trading partner is in decline, then it's unreasonable to think our own economy will not suffer. The potential for rising unemployment and a falling standard of living clearly exists. Going into a period like this low on cash and high on debt would be a big mistake. Too many people have not lived through a downturn to be afraid enough of debt; too many of us still believe that paper means wealth.

A personal financial plan is essential. There is no time to spare. A personal survival strategy follows.

In any successful financial plan, Step One is to analyse what you've got. This is like an inventory of your kitchen or workshop. Without ingredients or tools, you can't make anything. Without assets or cash flow, you're not going anywhere.

But even people who think they have a lot may find out they've got too much of the wrong thing and have left themselves vulnerable to inflation or recession or whatever comes down the tube.

So you have to calculate your net worth, which is also known as your wealth—it's simply the amount by which the things you own exceeds the debts you've accumulated. The Statement of Net Worth included here will determine several factors. It will act as a scorecard in your march to independence. The bottom line is to make your wealth grow as fast as possible while you keep risk within your personal tolerance level and minimize your taxes.

The net worth statement will also let you analyze your asset mix. For example, if most of your net worth is in the form of equity in your house, you are vulnerable in a recession, when real estate values fall. If most of your wealth is in Canada Savings Bonds, guaranteed investment certificates (GICS), RRSPS, Treasury bills or other liquid things, then you are vulnerable during a resurgence of inflation, when money falls in value. A rule of thumb: You shouldn't have more than three or four months' worth of income in paper investments like these, unless they are producing a good after-inflation return.

Similarly, the net worth statement will make you face your debt load. Remember, you are almost certainly better off financially to lower your debt than you are to increase your assets, because right now the return on money is far lower than the cost of servicing a debt. Bank accounts are paying, typically, less than 6 percent, while mortgages are 11 percent or better. Worse, your interest is taxable, while your mortgage payments must be made in after-tax dollars. The effect of higher taxes—the inevitable result of federal tax reform (more on that later)—is really to make debt much harder to handle. So analyze debts: determine which are long-term, like a mortgage, which are short term, like a bank loan, and how much you have on revolving credit with your charge cards.

Beside each debt write the interest rate on it. Compare that with the yield you currently get on investments. You'll quickly realize you'd be better off taking your assets and simply applying them to the debt, as painful as that may first appear. If some of your assets are growing faster than the cost of maintaining your debt (unlikely for most of us in the current environment), then use the poorer performers to pay down your loans.

Of course, one common way to increase your assets is to borrow money. A lot of people did that before Black Monday, to put in high-flying mutual funds, creating a tax shelter at the same time they made an investment. Such leveraging can be useful, but it comes with a significant element of risk. And if it pushes your total debt load past 20 percent of your take-home pay, then you're steaming for trouble.

So aim for this:

- Stabilize your asset mix. Right now I recommend ceilings of 20 percent cash, 10 percent precious metals, 40 percent real estate, 10 percent depreciating assets like cars, 10 percent stocks and 10 percent other appreciating commodities, like art and antiques (especially Canadiana).
- Maximize the return on your investments. There's no reason why your cash should be sitting around in low-paying savings accounts when it can earn more in a term deposit, GIC or Treasury bill.
- Minimize the expense of your debts. Eliminate mortgage debt through shorter amortization, prepayments or weekly payments. Take some cash and pay off bank loans and revolving credit cards.
- Make your assets work harder. If you have 100 percent equity in your house, consider investing some of it in more real estate. The interest on a new mortgage would be completely tax-deductible if you earned some income by renting out

STATEMENT OF NET WORTH

Date ______________________

Category	Item	Current Value	% of Total Assets	
Liquid Assets	Savings accounts			
	Chequing accounts			
	T-bills			
	Insurance value			
	Total liquid assets			
	Term deposits			
	GICS			
	Savings bonds			
	Other bonds			
	Stocks			
	Mutual funds			
	RRSPS			
	Precious metals			
	Other			
	Total investment assets			
Personal Assets	Your house			
	Cottage			
	Other real estate			
	Furniture			
	Automobiles			
	Art, antiques			
	Other			
	Total personal assets			
	Total Assets			

Category	Item	Current Debt	Interest Rate	
	Credit card balances			
	Car loans			
	Personal loans			
	Investment loans			
	Taxes owing			
	Total short term debt			
Long Term Debt	First mortgage			
	Second mortgage			
	Other			
	Total long term debt			
	Total Debts			

Total Assets	
minus **Total Debts**	
equals **Net Worth**	

the property.

- Get more investment cash from your cash flow. Reduce needless discretionary expenditures and start channelling money into other areas, like a regular program of accumulating gold or silver wafers. You might also try budgeting, which I find intensely boring, but which many of us need to do more of. Challenge your lifestyle assumptions and recognize that you can be an investor or a consumer but rarely both.
- Assess your risk load. You can afford to speculate when you're in your thirties, but in your fifties the focus should be on a long-term, retirement-oriented investment portfolio.
- Realize that your best assets are the ones you control yourself—something successful entrepreneurs and business people have long recognized. While personal tax rates can still approach 50 percent (don't believe everything Mike Wilson tells you), corporate taxes have actually been reduced. The federal rate is now 12 percent, and provinces add on, typically, 10 percent more. That means a small business is in a much better position to retain cash than you are. Incorporated companies can reward their owners with lightly taxed goods and services. Sure, the risks of independent business are higher than those involved in just taking a salary, but the rewards far outstrip them.

Take this book to the office and make a few copies of the Statement of Net Worth. Complete one every six months. Make that bottom line grow.

Now, your course of action should be something like this:

- Calculate your net worth.
- Analyze it, determining what percentage each kind of asset accounts for. Also look at total debt and the benefit it is giving you. Residential mortgage debt, unless your house is appreciating rapidly, is a drag. Investment loan debt, which is generating income, is not.
- Then analyze your cash flow. See where income originates and how expenditures line up. How much of your spending is necessary for lifestyle support and how much is discretionary? What are you wasting? The easiest way to increase your net worth is to curb spending. The smartest way is to eliminate debt. The hardest way is to increase income.
- Set your goals and priorities, along with a timetable. You can aim for your fortieth birthday, for retirement, for your kids' graduation or any other personal milestone. Establish targets for net worth, for income and for achieving a debt-free status. One of the first goals should be to pay off the mortgage on your house. That stabilizes your personal costs, then allows you to borrow against your equity for investment (and write off the mortgage interest).
- Determine the financial strategies you'll need for getting there. Think about how much tax you'll pay; what your investments are earning; and new opportunities.
- Then do it. Stop thinking about financial action and *take* some. You bought this book, right? Well, do something with it.

Get serious about planning for taxes. Realize the true cost of debt and take some assets to pay it down. Try to make all interest tax-deductible. Make investments according to your preferred level of risk, ranging from T-bills, bank accounts, Cannie Maes, term deposits and GICs, through bonds and real estate, to stocks, mutual funds and precious metals.

At all times, keep an eye on current economic conditions.

Right now it makes a lot of sense to

minimize your investment risks by going to high-yield, quality stuff like T-bills and mortgage backed securities. If a recession comes along, there will be big buying opportunities, particularly in the real estate market. Under the new tax laws, most personal exemptions and deductions are history, so it's more important than ever to shelter what income you can, and that means going for an RRSP.

Some other personal guideposts:

- After establishing what you have with the Statement of Net Worth, make a real effort to shift wealth from the "personal assets" column over to "investment assets." This is crucial for long-term growth. Investment assets earn you more wealth while personal assets, at best, just hold their value against inflation. Investment assets produce cash flow, but personal assets do not. In fact some, like furnishings and cars, steadily depreciate in worth.
- Always strive to invest in assets that appreciate in value rather than depreciate. That means putting money into antiques rather than new furniture, or investing in real estate rather than a new car.

  Consider leasing assets that you need and that are certain to fall in value—like your car. Use your savings instead to generate investment income.
- As mentioned, try to make as many of your debt payments as possible tax-deductible. With any loan taken for investment that will generate taxable income, you can write off the interest expense. But don't borrow to invest in high-risk items like many current equity-based mutual funds. If you want a fund investment, today's best bets are mortgage or money market funds.
- Even though cash is king during a recession, don't keep too much of your wealth in the form of liquid investments. The value of paper money is still, in the long-term, falling.
- Don't allow your debt load to creep up. Don't borrow to buy assets that will fall in value. Don't increase your mortgage to furnish your home. Don't add mortgage insurance premiums to your loan. Rent your television instead of buying it. Ditto the hot water heater.
- Increase your net worth most easily by increasing the rate of return on your investments; by spending less; by paying less tax; and by reducing debt.
- Taxes are the fastest-growing expense faced by Canadians. Make sure you maximize tax-free income by taking the equity in your principal residence when you sell. Take advantage of the $100,000 capital gains tax holiday while it's still around. Income-split with kids or spouse wherever possible. I know one guy who owns a farm and whose wife owns a city apartment. When he works in the city he rents the apartment from her, claiming it as a business expense against his income and giving her a gain.

  Defer taxes through RRSPS. Consider incorporating a company and getting your employer to pay you through that, or shelter supplemental income by running it through the company. Try to get your boss to pay you in other ways than just salary—with an expense allowance, club memberships or (best of all) equity in the company.
- And realize that financial planning is more important to you than a salary increase. Take a little of the time you give the boss and work for yourself. After all, you'll never achieve financial independence if you don't start thinking independently. Right?

So go for it.

Chapter Three

Real Estate and the Road to Redemption

The single theme of this book is the importance of achieving financial independence. And if you want a single path there, it's real estate.

This is not a definitive book on real estate (I already wrote one of those), but this chapter is going to give you a pretty decent flying lesson. Most of what I know has been learned through direct experience. I have learned that, in general, vendors are greedy and buyers are cheap. Realtors have one of the most frustrating jobs in the country. But there are also a lot of agents who, wet behind the ears from their too-short training course, mislead people about the biggest investment of their lives.

I have learned about mortgage companies to which I wouldn't refer even Richard Nixon. And I have learned that large, institutional lenders can, and sometimes do, show real compassion for the little guy. I've seen speculators make a lot of money. And I've seen them get their tails burned when the thought of profits wiped away their vision. Mostly, I've seen enough to convince me that real estate should form the cornerstone of most Canadians' personal financial plans.

Over the years I've made a lot of investments, in stocks, bonds, precious metals, start-up businesses, antiques and so on. But nothing has come close to giving me the kind of return that real estate has. Real estate now accounts for the bulk of my net worth, and I am actively pursuing more properties. As I write this, for example, I am trying to acquire a piece of real estate that I believe will carry itself and give me a place I can base my business. This is a good example (should I pull it off) of how you can come to control a big asset with relatively little money.

The property consists of a large single-family home built in 1918 and extensively renovated in 1980. Beside the house is a small structure of about 500 square feet, which has been standing for over a hundred years. Four years ago this was converted to a deli with a full kitchen and was connected to the house. At the same time the two front rooms of the house were turned into a craft shop. The property is zoned as both residential and commercial, and it sits in a good tourist town. Behind the house is a small barn with a two-bedroom apartment upstairs.

The vendors are motivated—they are of retirement age, and the husband is quite ill. They've already bought another home, in Nova Scotia. And the daughter who ran the deli for them has decided to move out and get married.

The asking price: $425,000. Right now the listing agent is offering it to me at $350,000. But I think the deal will filter down to about $300,000.

How can I swing that with only about $20,000 in cash? Easy. I stick to my first rule of real estate investing: Buy for cash flow.

The apartment above the barn rents for

$600 a month. The house can be easily, and legally, duplexed. The downstairs needs a bathtub installed where washer and dryer are, beside an existing two-piece bathroom. Upstairs an ensuite washroom will be taken out and a galley kitchen put in. The only other renovation is a separate entrance to the second floor. The total cost of doing that will be less than $10,000.

Now, each apartment will rent (in a flash) for $1,000 a month, so with the barn apartment, the property can give me $2,600 a month, with tenants paying their own utilities. That means I can carry almost $260,000 in financing, assuming I can get money at 10 percent.

In addition, there's a lady who wants to open a florist shop in the bottom of the barn, which has new hydro, plumbing and a separate septic system. The income from that is uncertain, but $500 a month is certainly reasonable. That would bring the monthly cash flow to over $3,000, meaning that at $300,000 the property would be self-sustaining. But how am I going to structure an offer?

First I visit my bank manager, Bob Hope. I arrange with him a line of credit for $60,000, with the option to go to $100,000. Last year Bob gave me $200,000 to swing a deal, and I was able to pay him back in about four months. Earlier this year I lined up another $70,000 for a real estate project, but was able to finance things out of regular cash flow. After those two experiences, I'm good for a lot of money with just a phone call. Above $50,000 and Bob has to call down to head office. But H.O. always says yes. So far, anyway. This, by the way, is not preferential treatment. I get money because I pay it back, and have given the bank reason to trust my judgement. I have also worked on this relationship. When Bob came to the branch, I made a point of meeting him. I also make sure he has in his hands, at least once a year, an up-to-date financial statement. The bank follows my personal net worth and the balance sheet of the company I use for making real estate investments. It is definitely worth the effort.

So I have $10,000 cash and $60,000 more if I need it. I intend to buy this property for $125,000 less than it's listed for, and I want the vendor to take the deal. I know that with a low-ball offer they'll sign it back to me with a higher price. But I also know they are very anxious to sell. The deli is closed, and it happens to be the middle of January, when the real estate market is dead and buyers are few and far between. It is clearly time to strike.

I'll probably offer about $289,000, anticipating a sign-back of $350,000. I will raise the offer to $299,000, and the sign-back will probably be in the $315,000 range. We will saw it off just above $300,000.

I will offer $10,000 with the offer and $40,000 more on the day of closing. That will give the vendors $50,000 cash, plenty enough to close their deal in Nova Scotia. Then I will ask them to take back a first mortgage at 10 percent, for $250,000. My agent, who presents the offer, will tell the vendors they're damn lucky I exist. Here is a man willing to go for an early closing, giving them $50,000 cash and then a guaranteed monthly income of $2,500 for the next three years. Where else are they going to get 10 percent on their money? And if they need the cash, they can always sell the mortgage to a broker. Simple.

My offer also comes with several conditions. I have gone through the house and the deli, meticulously recording every appliance and piece of equipment in there. My offer is conditional upon an attached list of items being included in the same price—things like microwave ovens, stoves, meat and pastry counters, ice cream machine and coolers.

I also make the offer conditional upon them giving me a list of suppliers for their food operation and opening their financial records for the past three years. Additionally, I ask to be able to view the property prior to closing with the intention of leasing the new apartments I'll quickly create. I ask, of course, for vacant possession, with the exception of the barn tenant, and I make the offer conditional upon being able to view the property on the day of closing. I do this to make sure that all the equipment on my list is, in fact, left right where it is.

These conditions are important parts of the offer. During negotiations over price I can, if necessary, start eliminating them to get the deal I'm after. I've included on my list some equipment I don't even want just so I can strike it from the offer. And I don't really care about the financial records. But I do care about the price and the vendor take-back mortgage. No bank's going to give me the 97 percent financing I'm looking for here.

I am confident this offer is going to fly, because the mood of the vendor is right and because others who have viewed the property have failed to see its cash flow potential. When the dust settles I expect to have a property that costs me $2,500 a month in mortgage payments and $345 to service the line of credit. But it will generate $2,600 a month now and over $3,000 when the florist moves in. So, with $10,000 down and another $10,000 in renovations, I will control a $300,000 property—probably worth more—and be in positive monthly cash flow.

But there is something even better about the deal: I will also have purchased a business. The deli is fully equipped and recently renovated. It is connected to the vacant front rooms of the house, and there is a crying need for a quality restaurant in this location. This is a business I intend (if the deal works) to own. And the money it earns will be pure gravy. This cash flow will go first into paying the bank off as quickly as possible (so Bob will lend me more), and then will be applied to the mortgage, which is fully open and payable at any time.

This isn't no-money-down real estate, but it's close. However, the deal makes sense because it has an assured cash flow and will generate enough business income to steadily retire the outstanding debt.

Most of the no-money-down jerks who make a living giving lectures (instead of buying real estate) miss this important element. They simply try to get a property that is marginally positive in its cash flow and then wait for escalating real estate prices to make them money. Personally, I think that is stupid and dangerous. It leaves the buyer fully exposed to many problems. What happens if mortgage rates explode? Or how about a tenant who refuses to pay rent or to move out? In a province with rent control legislation, it can easily take six months to get rid of the scuzzball. And what happens if the whole real estate market takes a dive? That's sure not out of the question. Recession, after all, could be just around the corner. With Canadians overextended and low on savings, the housing market could suffer a short-term decline. I am confident that my highly-leveraged properties can survive, but many others are going to end up on the auction block.

Real estate can be a powerful commodity. Over the long haul, the value of land and buildings continues to rise. The day you buy a piece of real estate you are on the road to a capital gain. If the property is one you live on, that gain will even be free of tax. And investment properties are even sweeter. Not only do you get capital appreciation but you get income as well. That money can be used to cover your costs and to finance other properties. If you own a home, you can borrow against the equity in it to raise the downpayment on an investment property. And because that investment is income-producing, the interest on the mortgage is tax deductible. You end up with an investment and with a mortgage that doesn't cost you anything.

There are several points to remember when trying to pull this stuff off. You must select the right property to buy, construct the best possible deal and then pay careful attention to the financing. And you must have the ability to see potential in a piece of real estate. I have a good example for you.

For six years I lived in a stone farmhouse on twenty-six acres. On the farm next door lived an aging spinster. Her barn was falling down and her house was a rotting, insulbrick-covered mess. But her land—fifty acres—was beautiful. The fields rolled and one portion of the farm was dominated by a huge glacial drumlin. In the back there was bush and a natural pond. The house was surrounded by towering pines and beside it was an ancient apple orchard. This oasis was just forty-five minutes from the corner of King and Bay in the heart of Toronto's financial district. The property was not for sale, but one we asked our neighbor if she wanted to sell. It turned out the farm was in the name of her dead father's estate, and the approval of an American sister was needed. So we invited them both over one day, and we had an offer ready for signing. After a couple of hours, we'd made a deal. The deal of the century, it turned out. We paid them $100,000 cash. Just before closing the land was appraised for $125,000, with no value assigned to the buildings. We'd already made $25,000.

A real estate boom was just starting to build. Now eighteen months later, a seventy-three acre parcel of vacant land next door is listed for sale at $270,000. One just down the road, a hundred acres of raw land, is listed at $599,000. We are, you see, in the path of development—subdivisons crawl closer each year. Eventually this land will go for housing, but our idea was first to maximize it, and gain a nice place to live at the same time.

The original plan was to just drive a truck through the house. This was no handyman's special. This was worse. Several families of squirrels lived in the uninsulated walls. Wildlife filled the dirt basement, and weather came in through several holes. The woman lived in three rooms, and the walls upstairs were fashioned from cardboard boxes. The kitchen was one sink, without counters or cupboards. Two wheezing, polluting oil space heaters were fed by a tube running across the floor, through a window and into a tank outside. The house was structurally a piece of garbage. Outside, the porches leaned in several directions. Every eavestrough was rotten through. Plastic sheets covered broken windows.

A condition of the sale—perhaps the one that clinched the deal—was to let the lady live on for several months after closing until she could find an apartment to move into. Meanwhile we attacked the outside. A guy was hired to trim the dead wood out of the thousand feet of trees on the road frontage. A new drive was constructed from three hundred feet south of the house, curving through the orchard. A berm was built over the existing driveway, which ran, uninspiringly, straight to the house. Sod was laid and trees planted. Then a split rail cedar fence was built across the frontage, requiring 120 posts and over 600 rails.

Finally, our neighbour found another home.

The day she did, I wandered over with the nine-pound axe I use to split firewood. I took aim at an interior wall—wood panelling below, lath and plaster above. A few whacks told me several things. Charred timbers were evidence of a serious fire in the building's life. And the laths didn't run in the continuous strips common in old houses. Instead this was split lath—large,

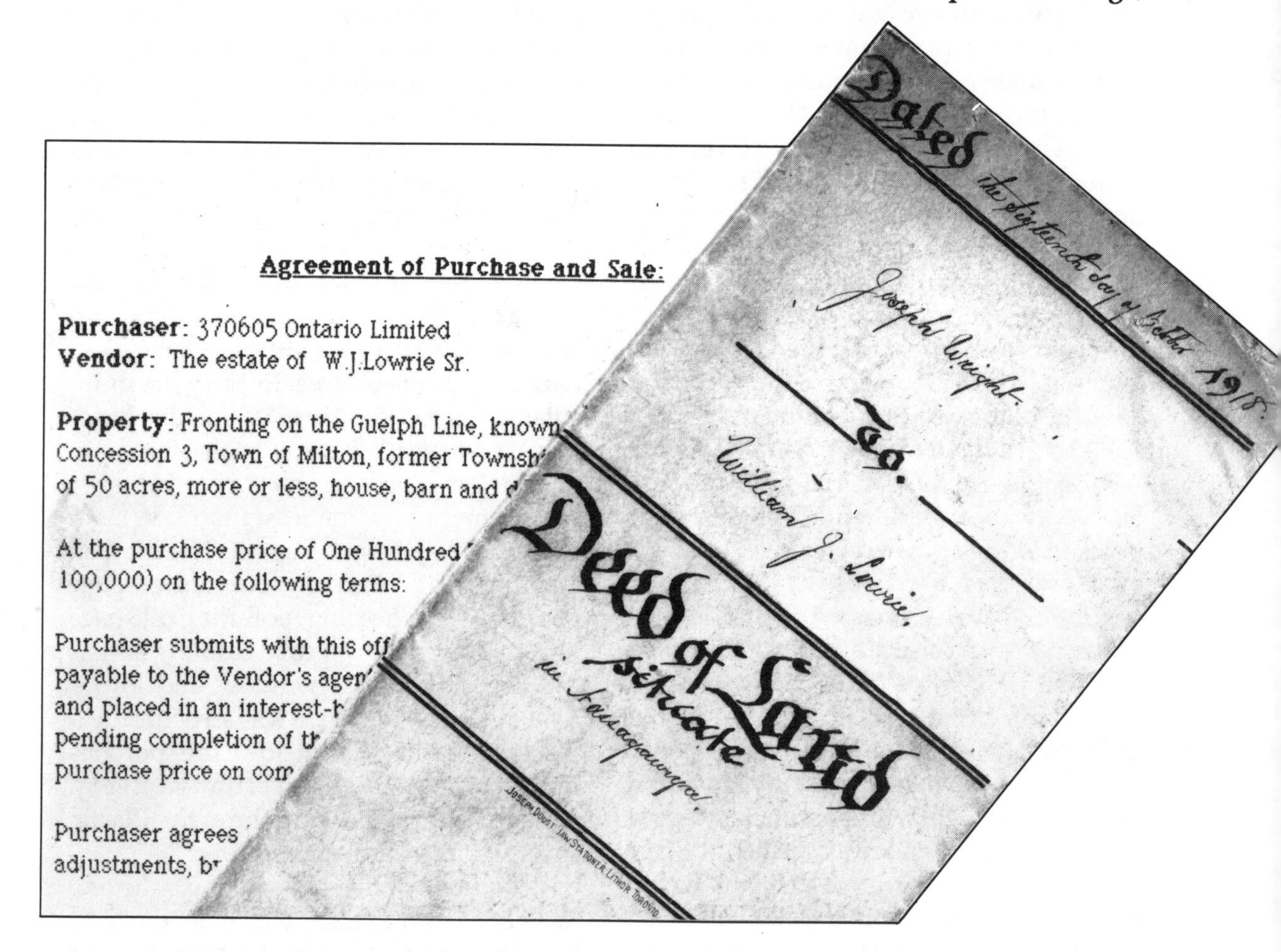

Agreement of Purchase and Sale:

Purchaser: 370605 Ontario Limited
Vendor: The estate of W.J.Lowrie Sr.

Property: Fronting on the Guelph Line, known
Concession 3, Town of Milton, former Townsh
of 50 acres, more or less, house, barn and

At the purchase price of One Hundred
100,000) on the following terms:

Purchaser submits with this off
payable to the Vendor's agen
and placed in an interest-
pending completion of th
purchase price on com

Purchaser agrees
adjustments, b

Dated the sixteenth day of October 1918.
Joseph Wright
To
William J. Lowrie.
Deed of Land
situate in Nassagaweya
Joseph Doust Law Stationer & Lithor. Toronto

This 1918 deed transferred a 50-acre parcel, more or less, from Joseph Wright to William Lowrie.. Fifty-eight years later I bought the land from Lowrie's daughter in a private deal, and found out that I had purchased an extra five acres. A five-acre lot a year later was selling for what I paid for the fifty. I drew up and printed this offer to purchase on my home computer. I usually use an agent in my real estate dealings,but the delicate nature of this one precluded me bringing in a third party. Besides, I wanted to be close to this deal, and make sure the vendor was well-treated. It's one thing to buy astutely. It's another to take advantage of a neighbor.

thin sheets of wood had been cut like an accordion, then stretched over the studs and plastered. This dated the house to at least the 1850s.

Then I uncovered something unexpected—a 12-inch-square hand-hewn pine beam. Several hours later I stood in a pile of rubble, looking at where this beam connected with an exterior wall. What I saw was another beam, running vertically. They were notched together and secured with two hardwood pins. This was classic post-and-beam, exactly the construction of most century-old wooden barns. It meant this part of the building was at least 150 years old—it was a pioneer's cabin, built in an historic and riveting fashion.

Clearly, taking this building down would be irresponsible. It would be a crime against local history, and it would be a missed opportunity.

The adventure had started.

In December of 1918 the northwest half of the west lot of Lot Number 31 in the Fourth Concession of the Township of Nassagaweya sold for $4,800, and William Lowrie—who signed for the land with an "X"—moved his family in.

Carved out of wilderness by surveyors for the Canada Company in the early 1830s, the lot lines had been approximated by eye, so that the farm covered fifty acres, more or less.

Sixty-eight years after Lowrie took over the land from widower and farmer Joseph Wright, I bought it, complete with the original stone surveyors' monument buried in the back fence line and the rotting wooden house at the front.

Because of the delicate nature of this deal—we were displacing a woman who had lived here all her life, the daughter of William Lowrie—I strayed from one of my chief buying rules and did not use an agent.

The way we found her. Squirrels in the walls, mice in the ceiling, porches ready to collapse and rotten wood everywhere. I swear the insulbrick was holding it together

The kitchen. Yes, all of the kitchen. In fact, this constituted just about all the plumbing in the house. Very low-maintenance.

The barn had natural ventilation. The drive-shed at right was mercilessly put out of its misery by a motivated front-end loader.

The barn had all its rotten boards removed, and inch-thick hemlock nailed into place. Here it is closed inon time for the first snow.

I also quickly realized in an initial meeting that what was going to make this deal work was cash. For the two sisters, the thought of hard cash was more appealing than a monthly income. The kind of monthly income a take-back mortgage would generate didn't turn them on. So the deal would have to be clean, and it would have to be cash.

I offered $10,000 as an upfront show of faith and a certified cheque for $90,000 upon closing. The owner was allowed to stay on for a while, and I agreed, at my own expense, to test the well and the property surveyed. The survey cost me $1,090, and it revealed one of the best real estate deals I've ever had. The survey turned up an extra five acres! Suddenly the farm had increased in size by 10 percent. (Five-acre lots, by the way, are currently selling in the area for a minimum of $120,000.)

It took six months and two days to destroy and rebuild the existing house. This involved removing over nine tons of material, displacing several hundred mice and bringing happiness to several local tradespeople.

The process was simple. First the house was gutted, until all that was left were the structural beams and exterior stud walls. All interior partitions were removed. The porches were removed (joyfully, by my hired university students with a pickup truck and a thick chain). The back woodshed/summer kitchen was torn off. Then the damp and aging insulbrick was peeled off, exposing the original tongue-and-groove wood siding. Off came the rotten eavestroughs, soffets and fascias. Under one porch we discovered an underground cistern, about twelve feet deep and fifteen feet across. The original kitchen had been fed from this through an iron pipe and a hand-pump, the bottom of which still sat between the floor joists.

When the foundations were exposed, the oldest part of the house showed serious deterioration. The original wood beams resting on the rubble stone foundation were largely rotted out. So the house was jacked up, and new pressure-treated lumber was placed underneath, then coated in concrete.

Six layers of asbestos shingles were peeled off the roof, followed by the original cedar shakes. Most of the roof boards were thin and brittle. Inside, stripping all material from the joists showed they lacked any kind of lateral supports. Tree trunks, still covered with bark after 150 years, simply rested together at the peak and trusted friction to keep them that way. So off came the entire roof structure, replaced by two-by-twelve joists. This allowed a foot of insulation to be placed in the ceiling. It also allowed a cathedral ceiling, and gave solid support for new skylights. Every window except two was popped and replaced by efficient modern windows custom designed to match the originals.

The electrical service was boosted from 60 to 200 amps, and the house was completely rewired. Ditto for the plumbing—an upstairs bedroom was converted to a large washroom with laundry facilities. A kitchen was installed downstairs. A new pump, pressure tank and water heater were put in.

The house was then insulated on the inside, a vapor barrier installed and the walls completely drywalled. The exterior was entirely covered first with two more inches of insulation then by pine board and batten. All exterior wood trim was replaced, and the house was sealed all over with three coats of stain and acrylic caulking. Door openings were moved, a six-foot slider installed and the floor joists rein-

Here's the finished kitchen with new pine floors, the exposed original hand-hewn beams, and cupboards we built ourselves in a week for $700 after being quoted $6,000 by carpenters.

The siding gets a coat of stain, new windows are installed, the electrical and plumbing are finished. Still to come is a duplication on the right of the two-storey structure on the left, a wooden deck around the addition, decorative gingerbread trim on the gables, and landscaping.

forced. The floors were recovered in tongue-and-groove pine.

By the time the job was done, the house had been re-created. All that remained of the original were the structural members, two doors, two windows and a quaint dormer (which was rebuilt).

This was phase one, and it made the place habitable. We moved in, sold our existing home and invested most of the proceeds in commercial, income-producing real estate.

I go through all this to show that the cost of major renovations need not deter you from giving it a fling. The key is to be your own general contractor, which saves you 10 or 15 percent off the top. Also try to minimize labor costs. I paid three university kids $6 an hour to do most of the work. That compares with the going rate of $15 an hour for a laborer and $23 an hour for a carpenter. When you are merely ripping the guts out of a structure, any motivated kid will do.

This is what I paid to turn a $100,000 junker into a $400,000 (appraised value) piece of real estate:

Item/Service	**Cost**
Survey	$1,090
Grading (backhoe, bulldozer)	740
Driveway	1,952
Tree removal, trimming	1,500
Landscape	241
Pump and pressure tank	681
Structural work and windows:	
Material	14,648
Labor	6,942
Drywall	1,857
Drywall labor	3,029
Plumbing	2,092
Sandblasting (pine beams)	470
Electrical	3,280
Equipment rentals:	
(saws, sanders, etc,)	700
Doors and installation	335
Disposal	260
Barn lumber	776
Barn labor	674
Appliances	2,511
Bathroom fixtures	1,748
Miscellaneous materials	1,851
Student labor	5,252
Total costs:	$52,629

That wasn't so bad. Phase two of this job was to construct a large addition and three-car garage, which cost just under $110,000. Because that was new construction, the job was given to a local builder and was completed in four months. The property is now worth close to $600,000—and because it is my principal residence, the profit I make if I sell it will be free of capital gains tax. Then I'll look for a junker and do it all over again.

Where else could I buy a basically new house on fifty-five acres within commuting distance of downtown Toronto for $152,000? No place, is where.

The power of renovation is that it can create equity. There is real logic in buying what realtors hopefully call a "handyman's special." Virtually anything can be done to a structure to improve it. The most important thing a piece of real estate has going for it is, of course, location.

I like to dabble in rural and historic properties. There are lots of tired and discarded homes out there. But the same principle holds true for urban real estate: Always buy the worst house on the best street you can afford. The house can be fixed, modified or completely nuked, if necessary. The location will draw buyers when it comes time to sell. Most people are lazy and will pay through the teeth to stay that way.

They'll fork over extra for convenience like easy access to schools, shopping or public transit.

And they'll pay even more for prestige. A "quality" street means a lot in this consumption-conscious society. So an investment in an address, rather than a house, can make sense. Renovation is one of the fastest equity-builders I know of. Don't be afraid to get dirty!

So many properties, so little time ...

Real estate investing can be addictive. It can be fun. And sometimes it can punch your lights out. It's a big subject, and mastering it requires a knowledge of mortgages, real estate law, demographics, human nature and negotiating techniques—unless, of course, you're a natural, the kind of person who can look at a property and just *know* this is a no-lose, money-machine, atmospheric little gem. I've met a few people like that. Of course they're very wealthy, and one is in jail for being too successful in his own short-cut way. But within a year of getting out, he's going to be on top again.

Real estate is easy to buy. It's easy to finance. Normally it goes up in value every year. It can yield you cash flow. Or it can give tax-free profits. There is an incredibly well developed resale market. You can live in it. You can develop or renovate it. And they are not making any more of it, unlike platinum, junk bonds or, for that matter, folding money. Sure, new, serviced land does come on stream, but every time that happens, the guy who owned it when it was raw likely makes a killing.

So let's reflect on some of the guidelines that have come to dictate the way I go about my real estate investments:

• The most important asset of an investment property is its cash flow. Sure, you can find something that's obviously undervalued just to resell and take a capital appreciation, but those opportunities are few and far between. In a rapidly rising market it's possible, though, and during the great 1986/87 boom in southern Ontario a lot of flipping took place. However, a small mistake in timing can have disastrous results. The last person in the chain of a flip ends up paying too much—guaranteed.

And then there's Revenue Canada to worry about. Money made flipping properties is not considered a capital gain. Rather, it is taxed as revenue income, meaning you may lose 30 percent or 40 percent of it (depending on your personal tax bracket), seriously diminishing your return.

Nope, it's better to go for cash flow and long-term appreciation.

Buying a duplex or store or apartment building or plaza should be a cool and mathematical exercise. Figure out how much cash you'll need to put into the deal before you're getting a positive cash flow, relative to expenses. The less the downpayment, the better, because your financing costs are tax-deductible against the income you receive. Just make sure that, with a big debt load, the cash flow the building generates is secure. And ensure that the tenants you inherit, or find, are good-quality people. Get references and credit checks and conduct a thorough interview. A little work now can mean fewer hassles later on.

A nice rule of thumb: Try to be in positive monthly cash flow with 10 percent down. Try for a return on your investment of about 7 percent with about 20 percent down. Do that, and you've found a bargain.

• There are basically three kinds of property: residential, potential, and ICI.

Residential, of course, you know about.

Potential real estate is land that has a future. It can be renovated into something that will produce cash flow, or it lies in the path of development. It can be a great long-term investment, but you've got to carry it out of after-tax income. Typically, potential-grade real estate does not produce income when you buy it and takes more money to set up for income. Going into this kind of investment, you need a big bank balance or a friendly banker.

ICI means "industrial, commercial and investment," and it can include just about everything other than your principal residence. It is real estate that pays you an income.

The rule here: Buy your principal residence with your own money and a minimum of borrowing. And then work hard to pay off your mortgage debt. This is because it's paid in after-tax dollars, and also because all of the gain in equity (the profit when you sell) is absolutely free of tax. But when buying ICI, use somebody else's money.

• When looking for a real estate investment, take the blinkers off. Don't restrict your search to areas you're familiar with and ignore others. Most often it's people who live in big cities who fall victim to this syndrome. They fail to see how a piece of real estate in a suburban or near-rural area might represent better value. And that's often the case. The return can be higher on an investment in a secondary market because costs are lower and the purchase price does not carry a city premium. Remember, cash flow is the big thing. Let the tenants worry if they live or do business in the wrong location.

• Make constant use of vendor take-back, or VTB, financing.

This can save you tons of money while annihilating the need to jump through some banker's hoops of fire.

As I write this, five-year mortgage money costs close to 12 percent, which is almost three times the inflation rate, and a hell of a lot. But a person would have to lock their money away for four years to get a 10 percent return from a bank.

So, you can make an offer on a piece of real estate and ask the vendor to hold a mortgage at, say, 10 percent for three years. He gets a very decent return on his money. He has security, because if you don't pay up he can get the property back. If he needs to cash out, he can always sell that mortgage to a broker. And you get financing 1.25 percent below the bank's going rate. It's kind of a win-win situation. It saves the purchaser from having to pay $125 to an institutional lender for an appraiser, and it also means you can escape costly mortgage insurance on high-ratio loans. Because the mortgage is private rather than institutional, this insurance is not required. Try it on for size in every offer you make.

• One trick no-money-down advocates use is this: When buying investment property for which you'll be finding tenants, make your offer to purchase conditional on being able to view the place prior to closing for the purposes of leasing. Then go advertise for, find and approve your tenants. Have the deal close on the same day the renters will be moving in. Collect first and last months' rent from them and apply this to the downpayment on the property. It's simple, easy and effective.

• Here's an obvious one: Buy low and sell high. So how come everybody seems to be selling high and buying higher? Because they're probably smitten yuppies, that's why.

The move-up market, not first-time buyers, vastly fuelled real estate prices over the past year. Here were people selling for $200,000 houses they'd bought for $160,000 a year earlier, and then moving into $300,000 properties. They were able to justify vastly higher mortgages because the amount of equity they had remained about the same. Besides, wouldn't that new house be worth $400,000 next year? Maybe, maybe not.

But this is *not* buying low and selling high. This is mindless lifestyle-driven consumption. It's the way to guarantee enslavement to a paycheque and to a mortgage.

In 1981 I bought an unrenovated stone farmhouse for $135,000. By late 1986 it had seen a net investment of $200,000 and was appraised at close to $300,000. I sold it in the early months of a real estate boom for $330,000. Six months earlier I'd bought that fifty-five-acre parcel of land next door, appraised at $125,000, for $100,000 cash. After a quick $50,000 renovation that rebuilt the small original structure, it was habitable. Within three months, because it was in the path of development, the property was worth almost $400,000. There was more to come, too.

Meanwhile, with $200,000 from the sale of the first property, I bought a sturdy 10,000-square-foot commercial building with two tenants. A small store next door came with the deal. The purchase price was $370,000, and with a mere $10,000 into the property I was in positive cash flow.

The current rent is $48,000 a year. The tenants pay all utilities, insurance, maintenance and even my property taxes. I financed the deal with a $160,000 vendor take-back mortgage at 10 percent over two years, with monthly financing costs of about $1,600.

This gives me a positive monthly cash flow of $2,400, which is a return of 14 percent on my investment. Where else could I get a return like that? And in the first year of ownership, the appraised value of this property has virtually doubled.

That's buying low and selling high. I took one principal residence and, with a little creative financing, turned it into a new home, two commercial properties and a steady source of income. The timing—just going into an up-market—came to mean that within a year I had increased the net value of the holdings dramatically.

The downside: renovation and short-term risk. Doing this deal involved a temporary $200,000 personal line of credit. It meant having a lawyer pore over the commercial leases I was buying. And it meant dealing with tenants, who are naturally suspicious of big ownership changes. It also meant a temporary downscaling of personal lifestyle, moving from a finished house to one under construction, and being able to see what a property *could be*. But financially, the temporary chaos pays golden dividends.

• Don't be afraid to renovate, and don't renovate the wrong way.

It's quite possible to spend a lot of money on a piece of real estate, expecting it to appreciate in value, and only come away disappointed. Adding a swimming pool, for example, can cost a small fortune while actually decreasing the property's resale potential. A lot of people don't swim, or view the pool as a foolish whim in a country with ninety days of swimmable weather, or are dismayed at the costs of keeping it properly maintained.

The opposite is true of spending money on a fireplace, or improving kitchen or bathroom.

Here's how some renovations come to affect resale value:

The average cost of remodeling projects and the estimated return on that investment, if the house is sold:

PROJECT	AVERAGE COST	% GAIN/LOSS at RESALE
Add a fireplace	$4,500	+38
Add a full bath	10,600	+22
Add a greenhouse	19,300	0
Add skylights	4,300	-6
Remodel a kitchen	25,300	-10
Reroof	4,500	-15
Add insulation	1,700	-23
Add a deck	6,900	-20
Replace windows/doors	13,300	-25
Add a room	38,000	-28
Add a pool	25,000	-67

•Selling the right way is as important as not messing up when you buy. In a rising market it's quite possible to sell privately if you advertise widely and have a lawyer hold your hand all through the deal. But in normal or stagnant markets it's essential to use an agent. Find somebody who is a proven winner in your area and has similar kinds of listings. And don't try to save a bit on commission by going for an exclusive listing.

The system usually works this way: Commissions are not supposed to be carved in stone, although many agents would have you think otherwise. It is not uncommon to pay as much as 10 percent to sell a hard-to-market vacation property. With urban real estate, 6 percent is common. For that you get a sign on your lawn and exposure throughout the region on the Multiple Listing Service, or MLS.

An exclusive listing typically costs you 1 percent or so less on the commission. Cheaper, yes, but hardly worth it. For one thing, the house never gets the wide exposure possible with the MLS system. Buyers only find out about the property through newspaper ads or the listing agents's network of contacts. Clearly, there's much less potential for attracting competing bids (the best way to get a good price).

•Don't fall for one of the oldest tricks in the book—the unsolicited offer. In this scenario a real estate agent knocks on your door and says he has a client anxious to make an offer on your house. Initially you say no, then you're intrigued. You think about how much money you could get and what a nice property that would fetch you. The agent assures you he's got a man, but as a formality you've got to sign a standard listing agreement—which usually attaches a very high price to your real estate.

Then, typically, the agent's buyer changes his mind, or gets run over by a bus. The agent assures you other buyers will soon be at hand. Then you realize you signed a listing for 120 days, instead of 30 days like you should have, and you find yourself out shopping for real estate you probably can't afford. Then the agent inevitably cames back and suggests a price reduction because the property is not attracting offers.

The moment you agree, you've fallen into the trap. Now you have become an active participant in selling something you had no intention of letting go. And as you reduce the price you also reduce your options, because to move up you're going to have to use more borrowed money.

I have seen many people go through the whole cycle. In the end they sell at market value, pay 6 percent commission plus closing costs, and buy something similar, paying legal and mortgage fees, along with land transfer tax.

It's called greed. And some agents can play it like virtuosos.

•Don't make the classic mistake of underestimating closing costs, which can often amount to 5 percent of the total value of the deal. And this amounts to more than paying for the lawyer or compensating the seller for a full tank of oil. There's also mortgage insurance, which is mandatory on high-ratio loans, the cost of a survey (if you didn't think to make it a condition of sale that the vendor provide one) and the biggie: land transfer tax.

British Columbia recently joined Ontario in establishing a two-tier tax system that punishes those who buy higher-priced homes—an especial burden on first-time buyers. Now almost half of Canadian provinces impose this unwise tax. Its unfairness is accentuated in provinces that also have rent controls, which constitute an unfair subsidy to those who choose to be tenants rather than investors. Land transfer tax is calculated, and payable, on the day of closing. Without paying it, the property won't be registered and the deal won't go through. The tax also rises with the cost of the property.

•Certain market conditions demand certain kinds of offers.

During boom times, realtors don't even want to present offers that have conditions on them. The most common are conditional on the sale of an existing property, or on the buyer being able to round up satisfactory financing within a certain time. Also popular is an offer conditional upon the purchaser having a home inspector issue a clean bill of health to the home.

Traditional markets see lots of conditional offers. And often those offers have a clause allowing the deal to be firmed up within a specified number of hours should another bidder arrive. Slow markets are sometimes dominated by these offers because buyers have all the cards and vendors know that prospects are few and far between.

But when things start to move fast, conditions are among the first casualties. During the height of the 1986/87 boom in central Canada, for example, conditional offers were virtually unheard of. Instead, vendors were forced to bid on properties they'd scarcely had time to inspect and often in an auction-like environment where multiple bids turned the process into a circus.

In Toronto it became a too-common practice for listing agents to deliberately undervalue a property to encourage a rash of offers from excited buyers, who found themselves suckered into a highly competitive environment. The adrenalin pumped higher as the listing agent insisted all offers be presented at the same time—highlighting the combative nature of the event. I saw properties sell for as much as $180,000 *over* the listed price. And for more than they were worth, too. And I knew of houses where five or six cars would be parked in the driveway, each of them housing a bidder. Every few minutes a clutch of agents would run out, jump in a car and have their client initial a price change, before going indoors to present it again. This was not the way to buy a house. And those who did it that way paid too much.

Things tend to be a lot calmer in the commercial market, and here conditions are expected. After all, buying a business means having the offer conditional upon the purchaser being able to examine current financial records. Buying a multiple-unit residential property means the purchaser has to have access to the property before closing to show it to prospective tenants. Buying a commercial, retail or office building means being able to examine the existing lease before firming up a deal.

Sometimes conditions are a necessity, and a safeguard. For example, when buying rural property, it should be a condition that the offer will expire if a water test reveals a contaminated well, or if the seller refuses to warranty the septic system. And it should always be a condition that any structure you buy is not insulated with urea formaldehyde foam.

•One of the better innovations to come along in recent years from re-born financial lenders is the pre-approved mortgage. This should be a must for every first-time buyer and a useful guideline for others. It shows you easily what price range you can comfortably shop in.

All you do is visit a bank or trust company offering pre-approval, fill out the forms and then find out how much money the company is willing to give you. Add that to your downpayment, and you know where to start looking. The commitment costs you nothing in most cases, and it allows you to do something powerful: when making an offer, you're freed from including a condition on financing.

Or you can use pre-approval to be dramatic, and maybe get a better deal. Make your first offer conditional on getting satisfactory financing along with a low-ball price. When you get a signback, improve your price just a touch, but boldly stroke through the financing condition. Now it looks like you're really serious, willing to go out on a limb if necessary. It also looks like this is all the money you've got. And it usually works.

•I always like to have an agent working for me on the buy side. When my offer is presented, I like having my agent in the room with the vendor and their agent. And I like to have a partner in the negotiating process.

But I also never forget an important point: the agent is working fundamentally for the seller, because that's who will be paying the commission. This is kind of a funny system, but it's nation-wide. Broker and agent guidelines make it clear that in the case of a dispute, the realtor's allegiance is to the vendor.

It's useful to remember this when, as a buyer, you're feeling a bit pushed. Just write up the offer you can afford and that you think is fair for the property. Have someone deliver it for you, but make up your own mind.

•One of the hardest things to do when selling is to determine the right listing price. Too low, and you will be cheated out of equity. Too high, and you might turn away prospective buyers. The danger then will be that, even with later reductions, your property has become stale on the market.

This makes "comparables" essential. These are similar properties that have sold in your area in recent months. In most market conditions they give you an excellent idea of where your pricing should be. In a rising market they give you the floor; in a declining one, the ceiling.

Ask any agent who wants to list your house for a list of comparables. He can get it with a modest amount of research, using the Multiple Listing Service statistics. Get addresses and actual selling (not listing) prices. In some cities, local newspapers publish this information weekly.

If you want something even more professional, hire an appraiser. An agent is not an appraiser, so don't be fooled when one of those little cards offering a "free appraisal" of your property is pushed through the mail slot by an aggressive agent. A certified appraiser will, in most markets, cost you around $125 to value the piece of real esttate. Going that route could avoid a costly mistake.

And if you have several agents asking to list your house, do not automatically go for the one who offers the highest price. Experience tells me he will probably do the worst job—and have the least experience.

• Take as much time shopping for a mortgage as you do looking for a piece of property to finance. Over the past few years the country's big banks and big trusts have been shelling each other with new products in an ever-increasing mortgage war. Gone, thank God, are the days of the conventional closed, twenty-five-year amortized mortgage. Consumers have awoken to the fact that this kind of loan is a massive rip-off.

I mean, really, borrowing $50,000 and paying back more than $150,000? Give me a better definition of loan-sharking.

But that's exactly the effect of a twenty-five-year am. Worse, the interest is all front-end loaded. During the early years of the loan you pay back virtually none of the original money you borrowed—you're just paying the accumulated interest on the mortgage.

So make sure you are part of the new wave in mortgage lending.

Take no mortgage that does not give you a way out—a method of early or accelerated payment. At the very least, you should have the right to make an annual prepayment of 10 or 15 percent on the outstanding principal. Better than that is the ability to increase your monthly payments by the same amount, at your will.

And better still is getting a weekly mortgage. Your regular monthly payment is divided by four, and that amount is paid each week. But because there are more than four weeks in a month, you end up making the equivalent of one extra monthly payment a year.

So what? So, keeping in mind that weekly payment does not let interest build up as fast, you can pay off a twenty-five-year mortgage in about half the time. And that can save you a lot of money—like tens of thousands of dollars.

Or you can simply decrease your amortization until monthly payments are as big as you can handle. The shorter the amortization, the larger your payments, and the less you'll pay off in total. Short-term pain for long-term gain. Honest.

I've stressed the wisdom of using as little of your own cash as possible for investing in commercial, income-producing properties. Well, don't try to apply the same principles to your home. Instead, take steps to get the mortgage monkey off your back as soon as possible. Paying a mortgage in after-tax dollars is a complete drag. It raises the effective rate of interest by leaps and bounds. It helps to enslave you, and what all this investing is about is personal financial freedom.

Having a debt-free principal residence is part of that. It means you've stabilized your shelter costs and that you have a source of personal security. So forget everything you've heard about no-money-down real estate when it comes to your home. Go for the biggest possible downpayment and the smallest possible mortgage.

Don't ever, ever, borrow more than you need to swing the deal ao you can also renovate or landscape or (heaven forbid) buy depreciating assets like appliances.

Before you resort to that foolishness, stop to think about how hard it is to pay back a mortgage .

Instead, finance things like that out of regular cash flow, and only use a bank loan as a bridge if necessary. If you can't afford them, then you have obviously screwed up somewhere along the road—probably by buying more house than you can afford.

Don't buy a new home just because the builder is advertising a cheapo subsidized mortgage rate. The builder has probably sent a cheque to the mortgage lender, "buying down" the rate on the loan offered. Better you take the mortgage at the regular rate and have the builder give the cheque to *you*. Then you can add that to your downpayment and end up with a smaller mortgage. When the loan comes up for renewal, you'll thank your stars you did it that way.

Be wary of variable rate mortgages unless you happen to be the governor of the Bank of Canada and can directly set interest rate policy. Rates have been volatile this entire decade. In the wake of Black Monday and wild foreign exchange swings, there's no reason to think things are going to settle down. A variable rate loan may be short and it may be cheaper, but don't kid yourself: it's gambling. And I just don't know why anybody would want to gamble with their principal residence.

We can't leave the subject of real estate without touching on a few other points.

The first is that while I think real estate is an ace investment, it is still very possible to get your can in a lot of trouble if you don't do things the right way.

A few more words about no-money-down real estate are in order. This is a very appealing concept to a lot of people. On the surface, it seems fantastic to be able to purchase properties with just a tiny fraction of the price in cash. Yes, it is possible. I have tested it myself. But the less equity you have in a property, the more dangerous that investment becomes. When you're so leveraged, a change in the formula can destroy you. What happens if a tenant stops paying rent, for example?

In provinces with rent controls the law is skewed to protect the tenant while assuming the landlord is a diseased, greed-driven, callous, twisted individual. This flies in the face of democratic capitalism. It subverts the notion of private property rights. It distorts market forces, and it inevitably reduces the supply of rental housing. Just look at Ontario, where rents can't rise by more than 4.2 percent in a year, a rate lower than inflation in most of the province. Landlords can't evict tenants for something as simple as non-payment of rent. Instead there's a lengthy appeals process, which can drag the matter out for six months. Meanwhile the tenant lives rent-free and can ask for someone to represent his interests, also for free. And meanwhile, the landlord has to pay his or her own legal costs, gets no income, and has to keep up the mortgage payments. If this happens to be a highly leveraged property, the landlord's up the creek.

Then there's the problem of wildly fluctuating interest rates. In the wake of Black Monday, things have been pretty stable. But what's to prevent a rerun of 1980's, double-digit mortgages within the next few years?

Nothing. And a run-up in loan costs would be disastrous for the investor who used no-money-down techniques. So would a precipitous drop in real estate values caused by a recession. There's certainly a good chance of that happening.

In such a case the mortgage on the property comes to be higher than the property's actual worth, when very little cash had been used to buy in the first place. Just ask folks in Edmonton and Calgary how that feels. It is still possible there to get your hands on a property just by taking over the mortgage payments. Why? Because the local market never recovered from the 1982 recession, and people can rent more economically than they can own. Although Alberta does not have rent controls, the vacancy rate can run to 15 percent (compared with Toronto's 0.01 percent), and you can get yourself a nice townhouse for $400 a month (in T.O. it's $1,000). This is a good example of what can happen when equity is small and debt is large. Thousands of people simply took a walk, and a provincial government agency was left with oodles of properties on its hands.

Sure, real estate sophisticates can make no-money-down techniques work,but it's not as simple as it appears. In Toronto two mortgage brokers, a lawyer and a no-money-down lecturer publish a newspaper on just such techniques, called *Creative Financing Forum*. Personally, I find this offensive, misleading and self-serving. (That the past president of the Ontario Mortgage Brokers Association is a principal bothers me no end.) But if you want to get involved with this side of real estate, their paper is a good place to start. Just don't send me a letter some day asking for bail-out advice. The last time I looked, lunch still wasn't free.

Another problem is the "guaranteed" sale, a sales technique once employed by the big real estate companies like Canada Permanent to garner more listings. Nobody respectable touches it these days, but you'll find it widely used by some of the bloodthirsty franchise shop operations.

Typically, this is what happens: A homeowner collects the mail and finds a solicitation from a real estate company. List your home with us, it says. You can't lose. If we don't sell your house, we'll buy it! One company I know mails over a million and a half of these fliers every year to just one area of Metro Toronto. They keep on using this gimmick because it works—it pulls listings. It's a simple enough offer—you can't lose, right? But you can.

First, the homeowner is told by an agent that he can get a wonderful price for the property. Then he's told the company will buy it if nobody else does. An offer to purchase is drawn up, with a deposit of a dollar or two. The offer is voided if another acceptable one is made, which is fine. But this deal also says that after just four weeks on the market, the listing agent is given the authority "to adjust the asking price to reflect any change in the market value, in the event no acceptable offer has been received."

Any homeowner who signs that is an idiot. He gives away the right to set the price of the commodity he's selling. It means the agent can drop the price repeatedly, assuring that the property will eventually attract a buyer and the "guaranteed sale" will never happen.

This tactic stirs the blood of honest agents, as it should. It's really just a bait-and-switch scheme, and the provincial authorities who oversee real estate should ban it pronto. If you run into anything remotely resembling this, be sure to run everything past your lawyer before you sign it. And, while we're on the subject, don't hire the same guy who handled your divorce to take care of your land deals. Find a lawyer who specializes in real estate. You would not believe how many lousy lawyers there are running loose in this country.

Another minefield for buyers comes with the purchase of a new home. Since the 1982 recession, when builders were creamed, almost nobody has been putting up houses on spec. Instead, they are all pre-sold. That way the homebuilder knows he won't be left with expensive, unsold stock should mortgage rates rise or the economy go down the tubes.

This is all fine and reasonable, but the pre-selling has become a tad ridiculous. Now it's not uncommon for homes to be sold which are not yet built and for which no permits have yet been issued, in subdivisions which are not yet serviced and even lack municipal registration. The potential for screw-up here is immense. And because there are so many stages still to go through, closing dates are no more than educated guesses.

The results: Buyers have to wait up to a year to get their houses. During this time they are without the use of the $10,000 or $20,000 they put down as a deposit, and generally are not paid any interest on this money.

Sometimes the deals don't even work out because the municipality does not give its approval or orders changes in a subdivision plan that can eliminate some lots. In many cases, closing dates are pushed back, sometimes several times, causing great inconvenience to buyers.

Worst of all, builders have been insisting that buyers sign these weird, one-sided, unfair and dictatorial contracts. They give the vendor the right to walk away from the deal, arbitrarily delay closing or even substitute building materials and change the house plan. Some attempts have been made in some areas to clean up this kind of contract, but they're still out there.

Anyone who signs one of these deserves all the grief that will probably come. Again, before you sign it, take any contract to a good lawyer. Strike through the clauses that offend you, substitute wording, initial the changes and then present it to the person in the builder's sales trailer. If they refuse to accept it, you've just had a lesson in how they do business. Drive on.

Finally, one of the greatest dangers is getting overextended. Evidence of this is everywhere. Some markets in this country—like Vancouver and Montreal—have a serious affordability problem. Others, like Toronto, have a major crisis. To afford the average home in Toronto takes more than the average family income. Increasingly, the middle class is falling behind. Purchasing power is diminishing. The capital of speculators and bargain-hunting foreigners is establishing new values for land. This pushes housing beyond the means of a growing number of people. And in an environment like this, some folks are driven to reach too far too fast.

Then, of course, we have the Yuppie phenomenon of the house as showcase instead of a home. Huge and expensive homes are the industry standard now, complete with whirlpools, circular staircases and central vac. This is depicted as mainline housing when, in fact, it is being sold to people without the means to afford it. In this material world there's the temptation to overextend to be able to own these personal palaces. And money is easy to get now. Maybe too easy.

I know of mortgage brokers who don't bat an eye at 90 percent financing. Some of them will even give you the full purchase price providing, of course, that you have the cash flow to pay them back in massive monthly installments. And this is where the problem lies. We're in a pre-recessionary economy, very indebted, very service-oriented, very prone to correction. It is not the time to be heavily mortgaged. If that house can't be carried on one income in a two-income household, then it's too much house. Period.

The way into real estate is from the bottom. Buy a property that is cheap because it needs renovation, or it's in an as-yet untrendy area or it's a little further from downtown than you'd really like. Buy a house that lends itself to the creation of an apartment. Find a tenant and let him help you make the mortgage payments.

Remember, you make wealth by buying low and selling high. That's true for stocks or gold or soya bean contracts. It is certainly true in the real estate market in the late 1980s. Why so many people have forgotten that mystifies me. But at the same time it's typical of a generation that, above all, can't wait.

Shokku!

That means "shock" in Japanese, and it's the word they use when North Americans are talking about a "crash." Black Monday creamed a lot of investors here, but it was not much more than a deep hiccup in Tokyo, where the market remains vastly overvalued.

There's a good case for saying the next shoe may drop there, and when it does the high-flying Tokyo Nikkei index will be in severe shokku. It's not a matter of *if* this will happen. It's just when. As I said, 1988 may escape for political reasons, but 1989 probably won't.

I mention this here because Japan also has the most speculative real estate market on earth. Companies that produce nothing and pay no dividends have raced higher in value on the stock market just because they happen to control land assets. Housing prices are unbelievable by North American standards, with a modest bungalow on Tokyo's outskirts selling for $2 million U.S. Most middle- class families cannot afford homes, and most are unwilling to break a 21 percent personal savings rate in order give it a stab.

It's reasonable to believe that in Japan the stock and real estate markets will fall together when the inevitable correction comes. But can the same be said for here? What are the long-term implications for real estate if the current massive market shifts? Will housing prices fall, and equity be wiped out?

I don't think so. In the immediate future central banks will probably continue the course of easy money—printing more of it and keeping interest down in an attempt to moderate the effects of the stock market dump. Stable mortgage rates, maybe even lower ones later in 1988, will help keep the real estate scene active. There are a lot of bargain properties around, especially in depressed markets like Calgary and Edmonton. And in southern Ontario, cities like Brantford, Cambridge and Hamilton offer some real buying opportunities, especially for small-time investors.

You can find hard proof in the listings of the *Hamilton Spectator*. Hamilton is thirty-five minutes from downtown Toronto, where it is tough to find any shack for under $200,000. It's also about to get a direct rapid-transit commuter rail link with Toronto. Yet here are properties, grossly undervalued in the first place which can be had for little down and which put buyers into immediate positive cash flow. I guess to people living in Hamilton, these are fair market values. To people from somewhere else, they are ludicrously low.

This is just one example of how markets can get mixed up; how localized supply and demand can have a major effect on pricing; and how there are still bargains to be had, even in major urban areas.

People who take advantage of opportunities like these need not fear the future. When the recession comes, they will be nicely insulated because their investments were economically sound. They did not buy at the top end of the scale.

I wish I could say the same thing for people who "invested" in their principal residences, putting up vast sums of money and assuming even greater mortgages. In a recessionary environment, it will be the lucky Dinks (double-income, no kids) indeed who find both husband and wife can keep their jobs *and* their cash flow.

Beyond the next year or eighteen months, I think real estate will be hot stuff. One legacy of the stock market mess will be a changed perception on the part of small investors. Going is the fascination with mutual funds and other paper investments. Coming back is an interest in commodities—hard stuff. Land, buildings, antiques, even art. Why would a Japanese insurance company pay $50 million for one lousy Van Gogh painting? Why in 1987 did that country's central bank convert busloads of yen into several hundred tons of gold for the new Hirohito coin?

Because these people are not dumb. They know that paper will have its day and that, long-term, commodities are where it's at. The scramble has been on to use paper to acquire hard stuff while paper is still overvalued. Maybe we should all be thinking the same way.

There's real evidence out there that inflation will come roaring back. I guess it has to. What other alternative is there for coping with the Western world's awesome debts? We either print more money and inflate them away or we plunge into a new age of sackcloth and ashes, trying to pay them off. Remember, every week of the year Canada goes another $576 million into debt. That's $82 million a day, or $3.4 million an hour. And this is new debt. It comes on top of the billions we already owe.

So tell me, how is Canada going to pay off this debt? How will America? Or Argentina, Brazil, Mexico, Poland, the Philippines? Do all the banks and governments just forgive this money, wiping trillions from the book, rewriting economic history and destroying the asset base of the world's banks? Or do we just continue to increase the money supply, making it easier to keep up the charade of loan payments and giving some breathing time to dream up a better solution?

This is the course that the world is going to take, and it is highly inflationary. And since one of the best hedges against inflation is real estate, it makes great good sense to acquire more over the course of the next two years. If a recession hits and prices temporarily wither along with public confidence, then so much the better. If you only buy bargains now, you won't lose that much; and if you stay liquid, you can pick up some more.

Shocks on Wall Street will continue. Tokyo will tremble. The headlines will still be black and foreboding. Scared money will be looking for places to land, and in the new world that is just taking form, real estate—the ultimate hard stuff—will play a leading role.

You can't own too much.

He works for a sports stadium in Tokyo. At 53 years of age, he's always rented an apartment, but now it's time to buy.

What he found, however, was that buying was impossible. Land fever has done awesome things to the Japanese real estate market. The cheapest place he could find was a condo apartment, 800 square feet, priced at $260,000 U.S.—and it was 1 1/2 hours from Tokyo.

"There's something strange going on here," he told The *Wall Street Journal.* "I am seriously thinking of moving to Canada."

Now, Canadians should take a minute and think about this, and what it means. By Japanese standards, Canadian real estate is a steal. The yen has been pushed higher in value through massive trade surpluses. There is a sea of money in that country, chasing things to invest in. Increasingly, the chase leads cash-rich Japanese outside the country.

As a result, we are going to see a lot more investment in this country, especially when Japanese financial markets stumble. Already Japanese and Hong Kong money is a real and daily fact of life in the commercial and investment real estate markets. Look at the "investment properties for sale and wanted" classifieds any day, and you'll see ads placed by agents for Oriental investors.

The pace of this investment should show us that Canadian real estate *is* under-valued. Canadians feel deprived when the average middle-class family can't afford to live within walking distance of the downtown core.

In Toronto, for example, it's widely perceived that there is a housing crisis. Yet it is relatively easy for the average family with an average income to find housing within commuting distance. Maybe they can't live easily downtown, but they sure can within a 30-minute radius. The average middle class Japanese, by contrast, is landless.

In New York, the days of the average inner-city neighborhoods is long gone. Apartments routinely change hands for millions, and monthly rents of $2,000 are common.

A modest house outside Tokyo can fetch $2 million U.S. Land prices there rose by over 93 percent in 1987, with speculation rampant. The situation's become so bad, in fact, that the government has ushered in a 96 percent capital gains tax on land profits made when a property is held for less than two years. In many ways, in a Japan flooded with cash, land has become the new currency. It is closely bound up with stock market wealth on the Tokyo exchange. Investors regularly use the equity in their real estate to borrow against, so they can play the market. And companies which have large land holdings are bid higher and higher, regardless of their business activities.

The cost of housing in Tokyo for the average white-collar worker is staggering—at about ten times annual earnings. The same measure in Canada's most expensive city, Toronto, would put the average home at over $400,000, or more than twice current values.

Even more arresting are the bargains to be had within 60 miles of the financial hub of Canada. A two-storey, detached brick house, renovated with a separate garage and on a 100-foot lot can be bought in Cambridge, Ont. for less than $140,000. That is actually below the cost of physical replacement, and shows dramatically that Canadians have no idea what others must pay for shelter.

No wonder the Japanese are coming. Wouldn't you?

A year ago Ernest Hillen, editor of *Influence* magazine, asked me to write a story about living in the country. At one time I worked with Ernest at the *Toronto Sun*, and he knew I was a "gentleman farmer."

This is the story I sent him. It was published, and then picked up two months later by *Reader's Digest*. The response was enormous.

I include it here as a footnote to the general theme of real estate, for real estate is not simply an investment. It is a lifestyle. I choose to work in the city, but I can't stand the thought of living there. To the urban mind, this may make me look unstable. I write things like the following because they must be said.

I've been telling you here about the financial importance of real estate—how it should be a cornerstone of personal financial planning and how, in this country, it's one of the best ways to get wealth and independence. But there's more. There's the personal enrichment of life that a property can bring. This is priceless. This is what I am talking about here.

The snow on the side of the road had a heavy January crunch under my boots. I walked straight up behind the van, where its exhaust curled and rose slowly in the frigid air. Moving to the driver's side, I grabbed the handle and opened the door.

The guy behind the wheel was gray-haired and dressed head-to-foot in battle fatigues. Beside him a younger man wore camouflage pants and a red lumberjack jacket. They were drinking coffee from a big thermos.

"You were hunting on my land," I said. "Don't do that again."

The red jacket denied having done anything wrong, but I told them any fool could trace their steps in the fresh snow leading from the van, over my fence, down the laneway and around the barn.

They lied some more, then admitted to hunting, and said the former owner let them do it. But that had been a year earlier, and since then I'd fenced a thousand feet of road frontage, constructed a new drive, gated and padlocked it. These urban trespassers had hunted out of season and were now giving me a hard time.

I cursed, slammed the door shut and started walking back. Suddenly four men jumped out of the van. They pushed me around, knocked me down, kicked me in the stomach and then threw hot coffee in my face. For a few gripping moments I was sure it would get worse. One of the guys was huge, and if the red jacket hadn't held him back there would have been gentleman farmer's blood on the shoulder of the road.

I live on 55 acres 60 miles from the corner of King and Bay in downtown Toronto, and this roadside encounter brought into sharp focus some elements of the life I lead—the life of someone who inhabits country property without drawing financial sustenance from it; someone who knows the trials of such a life as well as its blessings.

One of the first things you learn is that travellers from the city don't seem to understand that private-property rules apply in the country. For them, fences are to be climbed; fields crossed; lanes marched.

You also learn that yours is a close community. Within 5,000 feet of that spot live a Metro Toronto cop, a novelist, a horse vet, an Air Canada pilot, an author-chef, former NHL star Lou Fontinato and musician Peter Appleyard. There are also a few farmers and teachers mixed in. If any one of them had been going by that morning I would have been helped. The day the goofs knocked me down, Mary Carley (she lives in Sir Charles G. D. Roberts' old house on the corner) brought me a red basket in her green Volvo. Inside the basket was chamomile tea, fresh eggs from her chickens and some home-made biscuits. It was a measure of the woman, but also a reflection of the community.

This is land clearly in transition. Last winter I sold a 26-acre parcel next door to a Bay Street stockbroker. I have lived here eight years and in the past 30 months six subdivisions have been developed within five miles.

One is being sold with boulevards and street lights—which I will be able to see from the top of the drumlin in my second-to-back field.

Soaring real estate values are forcing replacement of working farmers with white-collar workers—and every morning we drone together towards Highway 401, setting the cruise control at 120 clicks and waving back at the farmhouse.

It is an intense form of double life. Leaving home, it's only natural to wear a Co-op green coat, work gloves and snowmobile boots. But 50 minutes later you emerge in a world where people live in apartments, travel the subway and arrive at work in little shoes and flimsy, fashionable trenchcoats. And the trip home can see you arrive in a business suit, only to end up chasing goats out of the garden.

It is a life of forced exile. Work becomes city. "Leisure" is country. City people, you learn, are too lazy to drive out to the country. Country people are too paranoid (of the little shoes and trenchcoats) to drive to the city. For those of us who choose this life, and stick with it, there are moments of beauty that override that time when you have to rip open the door of a 1978 Ford van.

It is a world of dichotomies, contrasts and revelations.

Above all, there is the space. That, you will learn, buys privacy—a kind of unrelenting peacefulness that can breathe warmth into your soul. It is the privacy to step outside on a sunny May morning in your pj's. To leave your home and vehicles unlocked. To throw a ball for the dogs as hard as you can—in any direction. To hit 60 km an hour in your laneway. To chainsaw the hell out of anything you want, at any hour. To lie in the hay with your wife.

This is what urbanity cannot give you. And if you don't care about peace, space and privacy, don't even read the first Country Property classified.

The neighborhood here—and in most near-city rural locations—is varied, fascinating, friendly and supportive. We lend and we borrow—garden tractors, tools, sheep, food, advice and labor. Anyone who has lived in the country will tell you that the neighbors become friends. In the city, neighbors are often considered irritants. There are a lot of tall fences.

Gentlemen farmers also know they don't have to make a living from the land. Instead, they pay their dues on the highway and in the city. On weekends the land is there to soothe them. It affords natural exercise and the ever-present ability to work with your hands.

The day you have the place fixed up is the one the barn door will fall off. Build a rustic cedar rail fence and the horses will chew right through it. Mow the grass on Friday and Saturday afternoon it needs mowing again. The body can thrive in an environment like this. Often, it has to.

There are few pleasures more perversely satisfying than getting dirty, after a week of working in an office where a spotted collar is cause for real social embarrassment.

But here is also a life with adversities city folk are barely aware of. During the winter months there is that drive—with salt, shovel and warm clothes in the trunk—

with one ear to the weather bulletins and another to the traffic reports. There are tons of snow to remove from the driveway and there is the unique fury of drifting. Most of all, there is the need to become—almost at once—a rugged individualist. A rural renaissance man, able to fix the tractor so the snowblower will work so you can get the hell to the office.

Out here the rules change. You are only as good as your last post hole. You can farm with your chequebook, or you can do it with your hands. You have a new language to learn; of augers, balers, page wire. Respect in the neighborhood comes more from achievement than from social status.

I meet Peter Appleyard at an auction sale, where he's bought a mess of boards for ten bucks. I have my pickup truck, and he'd only got a wagon—half-filled already with his vibes. So together we load up, drive them home and unload, drawn close because we sweat together on a July afternoon. It happens this way. They may even have a name for it in the city—agrarian male bonding, perhaps.

Then there is the disillusionment I have seen on the faces of many who think they yearn for rural values when, in fact, they want a stone house on an estate lot with all the town services. They don't want to get dirty and they don't want to spend five hours cutting the grass. They pay to have it done—and they pay dearly. They are cash cows for the locals to milk.

On the other hand, I board horses, grow hay and sell it. There have been dabbles with sheep and such, but that's a major responsibility. Hay just grows, and there's a ready market for it. All that lets me pretend to be a farmer enough to claim a restricted farm loss against my city income. I can have dogs and claim their food as an expense. I can claim portions of mortgage payments, insurance, repairs and vet bills. If I lease my land to a full-time farmer I can get my property taxes rebated.

And, if I am very clever about it, I might even make money myself. Hay sells for $1 a bale when it's cut and sitting in the field. But in February it can fetch $2.20. City people who like riding are willing to pay $200 or more a month for a place to stash their horse. And, of course, you just need to buy land in the right place and then wait for the subdivisions to find you. Land here has doubled in value in the past 24 months. In five years it has tripled. The same is happening in a score of other similar areas, and the opportunity to gain wealth through real estate here far exceeds that in the city.

But is the gentleman farmer in it for Yuppie-like personal gratification and financial gain alone? That sounds convincing enough, but there's more. We near-farmers, we urban/rural, motoring complexities, we are not city slickers dabbling in another lifestyle the way you might swizzle a drink and then suck on the stick. We are also investors in a way of life that needs all the help it can get.

Sometimes, like Denison Mines boss Stephen Roman, we run corporate barnyards turning out superior genetic stock. Like my neighbor Louie Fontinato, we farm some marginal land back into production. Like Allan Burton, the former chairman of Simpsons, also nearby, we take a leadership role in local conservation. Like me, we have the satisfaction of turning acres of goldenrod into acres of crops.

These are not frivolities. They are personal contributions on a community level. They are as much a part of the face of farming today as the grain combines of the west and subsistence plots of the east.

And, the label notwithstanding, we are neither gentleman nor farmer. We are ourselves.

Chapter Four

The way of the entrepreneur

In 1975 I had a fine 1958 Jaguar sedan, British racing green with red leather upholstery. It flew down the highway, took great strength to steer and turned a lot of heads with its long, sloping front end. It was the kind of car you called "she." I drove it as my every-day vehicle. Dorothy, my wife, had a Volkswagen Beetle. I was editor of a weekly newspaper in Oakville, a rich town outside Toronto, and she was promotion manager for a shopping mall. For the first time in our marriage we had saved more than $5,000.

Early that year I was suddenly hit with an uncontrollable urge to do my own thing—be my own boss, run my own company. I was twenty-six years old and had no experience at being an entrepreneur. Hell, I didn't even know any entrepreneurs. My main family occupation was teaching, and my father had risen the ladder to be director of education in one of Canada's fastest-growing regions. Here I was, with a university degree in English literature, $5,000 and a '58 Jag. We both had good, secure, well-paying jobs. And a three-bedroom, three-bathroom townhouse. It felt like we had a lot to lose, and that the odds were high.

But that didn't matter. I was smitten. I didn't want to *work* for a newspaper—I *wanted* one.

In those days my parents owned a hobby farm forty miles away. The nearest large centre was Guelph, a then-sleepy Ontario city of about sixty-thousand people. It had one newspaper, a Thomson-owned daily that many felt was the worst in the province. It was produced with outmoded equipment, overcharged its advertisers and considered editorial material as worrisome wedges that kept the ads from scraping against each other. Even worse, with the name *The Daily Mercury*, it sounded like a diet supplement.

Fine, I said to myself, Guelph will do nicely. The first thing I did, as a working newspaper editor, was to write a letter of recommendation and get a friend of mine on the staff of the *Mercury*. His task: to learn everything he could and then report for duty to me in four months. He would be my editor.

I worked for weeks on a business plan—determining overhead, figuring out how little equipment I could get away with, coming up with advertising costs and a budget for salaries. By using newer technology, distributing the paper free to every home and concentrating on local news, I was sure a market niche could be found. The bottom line came out to be an overhead of $5,000 a week. I had no idea of what to expect in the way of revenue.

I talked Dorothy into coming on board with me; incorporated a limited company without the help of a lawyer; and then went looking for money. I found two equity partners—a sales rep on the paper I worked for and my father. Both invested

$10,000. My dad's money came as a loan without strings, and the other fellow was enticed into the deal after I offered to make him advertising manager of the new weekly.

After a long walk in the rain, we managed to come up with another $20,000. The decision: use all our savings and sell everything of value to raise cash. The Jag, too.

The night she went a guy came over, took it for a fast test drive, then came into the house. "I'm not even going to beat you down," he said. And he took a big wad of hundred-dollar bills from his pocket and threw them down on the coffee table. At week's end I was driving an Austin Mini. It felt like a mutant breadbox with a wheel at each corner—but I had $40,000 in cash, enough money to run the newspaper for eight weeks. If cash flow didn't take over from there, I was finished.

In hindsight it was the decision to use our savings, to take an investor and to not borrow to finance the business that allowed it to survive, despite inexperience and several obvious mistakes. Without a banker's axe hanging over our heads, we had some breathing space. Other creditors can always be danced around for a while, but not a bank.

On September 10, 1975, after staying up all night, our first edition was printed. The newspaper was housed in an old stone building downtown, which had been a fish and chip shop. (Two years later, it still smelled of halibut.) I had a staff of eight to start with, two stolen from the opposition, and several hundred carriers who were paid a penny and a half for every delivery.

Well, the business made money from the start, and everybody kept on getting paid. We worked hard at cornering the market for local real estate advertising by offering to print for free pictures of houses to accompany realtor's listings. Another of our secrets was ruthless attention to overhead. We shaved away every cent we could. With a new venture it was a hell of a lot easier saving money than making it. That meant buying used equipment, doing our own crude renovations, learning different tasks and not being too proud to lunch with the mayor and clean the office john in the same afternoon. Dorothy and I worked like dogs. And every week the product got better and the payables were easier to meet. After two years, it was even starting to look comfortable. Dorothy and I were just finishing the new home we'd built in the country, and the Austin Mini had been mercifully traded in, for a new Triumph TR6. Success, it seemed, was within our grasp.

Our inexperience had been overcome by enthusiasm, a well-tailored product and rigorous cost control. Meeting payroll was still a constant problem—but that was due more to advertisers being slow to pay their bills than to poor sales. Offering a hefty discount for early payment helped, as did a few phone calls. But in a small city—in fact, any community—you have to treat your customers well. You could be on the phone demanding money while your sales manager is coming through their door, looking for more business.

For the first six months we ran without a bank line of credit. Dorothy learned how to manage a composing room, where the newspaper was produced. I learned how to sell. Within eighteen months we were doing $500,000 a year and banking none of it. Every dollar went into staff and equipment. We bought computerized typesetters and expanded the building. We added editorial staff. We bought a delivery truck. We put color on the front page. Then we started another paper, to serve the rural area around the city. And then we began to run into trouble.

In the third year I wanted to expand, and I had the plan in place. Two weeklies were for sale in suburban Hamilton, thirty minutes to the south. We needed cash, more cash than the existing operation was generating. I made the biggest mistake of my inexperienced life: I took on a partner. In return for his cash infusion and banking connections (rich family), he got a portion of the business. Eventually we bought out the sales manager and became equal partners.

At this point the expansion became nearly mindless. We bought the papers to the south and then commissioned a new building. It was built to suit, on a long-term lease basis. We were responsible for all interior finishing and leasehold improvements. My partner professed some knowledge of construction, so he took over that project while I managed the bustling little paper empire.

One Saturday morning I wandered onto the new site and I was shocked at what I saw. The layout tables in the composing room were custom-made of oak, with laminated tops. The woodwork throughout was hand-finished pine. There was a boardroom with chair rail and colonial trim. We had a $700 waterfountain and expensive hand blow-dryers in the washrooms. The partners' offices were huge, and the heavy, solid doors had brass handles.

Immediately I ordered work stopped, but it was probably too late. We had commitments now that could only be satisfied with steep new bank financing. Naturally, relations with my partner deteriorated. I didn't want a fancy office. I wanted cash flow.

Three years after starting the business, I sold it—to my partner. At least his inexperience and bravado allowed me to walk away with a good chunk of money. His rich father rewarded his entrepreneurship by buying him a new Mercedes, but he would not put more capital into the enterprise. Within two years the business failed. My former partner was forced to put the company into bankruptcy, and one day the sheriff came and took away the equipment, the fancy boardroom table, the hand-made layout tables.

It was a classic small-business story. Although I was able to succeed in my own right, statistically this experience had been right on—failure within five years.

Why? Because the sound first principles had been violated. Cost control was sacrificed to ambition. Expansion came too quickly, and it was too leveraged. As the business rapidly grew, there wasn't enough management time to supervise it. As indebtedness grew, inordinate demands were placed on the sales staff to raise revenue in a market that could not expand as fast.

I chose my partner poorly and ended up with an individual who had misrepresented his credentials. I surrendered too much control. I, too, was ambitious. In many ways, I was too close to the business, working unending hours and not standing back from time to time for a longer view.

But I learned massive amounts. In a bit more than three years I gained thirty years worth of experience. Going from an idea to a fledgling beginning to a company with sixty employees and $1 million in sales, and then to walk away—that taught me much about the way the world works. It showed me that if a guy like me could do it, then hundreds of thousands of others—people who were employees—could do it, too. Despite the mistakes made, as an owner-manager, I probably had more job security than most people. I had control of my time and my finances. And this was in an economic environment far less volatile than today's. In the mid-1970s inflation, not recession, was the chief worry. In the late 1980s corporate employees are more mistaken than ever to think their jobs are long-term. Corporate rationalization—cutbacks, takeovers, mergers and buy-outs—have proven the days of steady year-over-year growth are gone.

Dorothy and I have since created, and learned from, other business ventures. In 1987 Dorothy expanded a small seasonal business she had been running—the sale of investment-quality Canadian antique furniture. This time the expansion was planned, and controlled.

We financed the venture out of cash flow from other business operations, primarily rent from commercial real estate investments. There was no bank borrowing, although I did arrange for a $50,000 line of credit as a routine precaution against the unforeseen. The security for that was an unsigned mortgage against property we owned. The market was researched, and the business moved to a tourist town which lies with in a thirty minute drive from over two million people. Operating costs were stabilized as much as possible. We bought a seventy-year-old Victorian brick house, hired student labor, and did the necessary renovations ourselves.

Every effort was made to promote the business—press releases to local papers, bagpipers outside during busy weekends and ads in newspapers and magazines. Meanwhile, overhead was controlled and cash was put into inventory and marketing rather than equipment or fixtures. And the formula worked. Weekly cash flow has been positive since the opening. Inventory levels have been expanded, payrolls met, suppliers paid within thirty days and all other commitments met. The business has no indebtedness, no outstanding payables and provides employment for two people. It's modest, but that's the way most small businesses start. Expansion must be controlled—a lesson I will not forget.

Currently we're expanding the building and the business by opening a cafe and patio. Two more jobs will come into being, while cash flow should significantly improve. The two sides of the business will complement each other—food service on one hand, quality (and often expensive) antiques on the other. Bridging the two is a selection of crafts, home fashion accessories, and jams, preserves, chutneys, dips, teas and dessert sauces.

The conscious effort here is to diversify rather than specialize, while maintaining top quality inventory. This will likely mean slower growth, and it means sitting on a lot of expensive stock. Fortunately, we're now in a financial position to do that. As long as cash flow handles operating costs, the business can take as long as it likes to turn into a retail conglomerate.

This is just one way of running a small business. Starting from scratch certainly carries its risks, and for that reason a lot of first-timers prefer to buy an established business or get into a franchise. And taking over a business is one of the safest ways of getting out of the corporate shadows and into your own sun. Some of the advantages include:

- Knowing what kind of income the business generates and what the operating costs are. In a start-up situation this can often be a total guess. Buying an established business means that somebody else has done the initial worrying.
- Being assured that a market already ex-

ists for the product or service. If it didn't, then the business would not be viable.

- Getting facilities, inventory and equipment at less than replacement cost. Almost always you can take over an operation for less than it would set you back to build it up in the first place. The seller has been able to claim depreciation, and the buyer gets the benefit of used equipment costs.
- Cash flow. Unlike a start-up situation, in which many weeks or months have to be spent in pre-opening activities, buying an existing business means enjoying an immediate income.
- Getting a list of suppliers who already have an ongoing relationship with the operation—people who are used to providing the business with the fuel it needs to keep going.
- Price. People sell businesses (like residential real estate) for different reasons. Some of them are tired, or old, or sick of working so hard. So there can be bargains found, and a good return on investment. Often vendors are willing to assist in financing, keeping the downpayment low. In a start-up situation you need cash, and usually lots of it.

Of course, there are also problems. To find them, try to pinpoint the reason the business is for sale. Some of the likely reasons:

- Financial trouble. Sometimes hard to spot, so make sure you have your accountant climb all over any numbers that a vendor gives you, looking for telltale signs. It could be masked on a balance sheet that otherwise looks healthy, maybe because an owner-operator has not included any pay for himself. Maybe those accounts receivable should be given proper funerals, because they're really bad debts.
- A poor location. A mega-problem for a retail operation. Maybe the community—the market—has changed, and the business has not. Maybe the demand for the product or service has suddenly dropped. Maybe new competition has forced the owner to bail out while the bailing's still good.
- Poor or old stock that can't be replaced because of insufficient cash flow. Or ditto for equipment. Maybe the real estate is in rough shape, and a lot of immediate capital is required.

You can score in buying a business, or you can get shafted. The key is to be exhaustive in your research. If you're going to buy a store, buy one you shop in, whose merchandise you like and know, and in a location that obviously works. And look hard at what you are actually buying—it may not be all it appears.

For example, a successful grocery, gift shop and food services operation I know has recently been for sale. The price was $200,000 plus inventory; the store grosses several hundred thousand a year, yielding a gross profit in the six-figure range and a net of about half that. On the surface it didn't look bad, but the business was a tenant in a building essential to its successful operation. Without that location, it would not be viable. The vendor has just over six years left on the lease. In other words, the buyer would spend $200,000 to earn roughly $300,000 in net profit over that time. But he'd also have to buy, and finance, the inventory. Unless the buyer could drastically increase the profitability of the business, taking it over would be a waste of time and money.

But in other instances a business can be bought for virtually nothing. Look at the purchase price in terms of the liquid assets that come with it—like cash in the bank and accounts receivable. That's money you can get back as soon as the business is secured.

On the other hand, be very careful that all debts against the business are revealed. If you do the deal, get the vendor to sign a declaration that says he bears some responsibility. If he won't do that, ask why.

Determining if the asking price of a business is fair is the hardest part. It's not as simple as buying a piece of real estate, because you have to put a weight on good will, inventory, equipment, staff, the products and services, location, market share, potential and existing competitors, cash flow and your potential to make something better than it currently is. You'll stand the best chance of doing that accurately if the business is something you understand, have experience in or are very interested in learning.

There are, at any one time, thousands of businesses up for grabs in this country. The "Established Business for Sale" classifieds in daily newspapers are a good place to find them. Also look for ads in national business papers like the *Financial Post* and *Financial Times*. Then there are commercial real estate brokers who may have many unadvertised listings. Decide at the outset what kind of money you have to spend, the extent of your financing and the kind of cash flow you'll need personally to get by. And concentrate on the problems a candidate business might have. After all, there are few valid reasons for somebody to sell a profitable, going concern. Still, it does happen. And it might as well happen to you.

At the end of this chapter, I've listed some books that may help you determine a course of action. To be frank, there are few decent ones around, and not a single volume that answers all the questions that should be asked. One of the best pieces of advice has to be to follow your heart. If you want it, go for it. Never let a '58 Jag slow you down.

For thousands of Canadians, being in business means getting into a franchise. This isn't surprising. After all, franchise operations are coming to dominate whole sectors, like take-out food. As soon as somebody comes up with a good idea, they see big returns by licensing that idea to anyone who can make it viable.

Simply put, a franchise is an agreement to do business under somebody else's name. You buy the right to operate in a certain area and in a prescribed fashion and often with prescribed materials. Here are some perfectly good reasons for buying a franchise:

- An overall lower chance of failure. If you get hooked up with, say, McDonald's, Speedy Muffler King or Holiday Inn, chances are that the company—because its image is at stake—will carefully select a business location for you and be actively concerned with your success. And because the company has been successful many times over, it knows what you must do to also be a success.
- The name factor. It alone can justify spending big bucks to get into a franchise. Consumers come to expect a certain product line and level of service from, say, a Canadian Tire store. They may be pre-sold before they walk in for the first time.
- Exclusive operating rights in a defined territory. The franchisor agrees not to license anyone else to operate nearby under the same name, so all you have to worry about is competition from other companies.
- Mega-bucks advertising, one of the main

benefits enjoyed by franchisees. A campaign for Shoppers Drug Mart is seen and heard by consumers over a huge area, and each franchisee reaps the benefits. None of them, on their own, could afford to buy that kind of publicity.

But all is not sweetness and cash flow, because buying a franchise can also be financially hazardous.

- The big problem is cost, which can be horrendous—McDonald's, for example, wants people with several hundred thousand dollars. And for that, you may end up just about anywhere in the country, working like a dog. Besides the initial fee there can be other heavy costs, such as buying equipment, or leasing operating space.
- Then there are ongoing royalty fees, which require you to hand over a specified portion of either the gross sales or net profit. The more business you do, in other words, the bigger the cheques you write.
- Some franchises come on the market with unproven track records and are very risky ventures. When buying, you have to research the company. Visit other locations, talk to other franchisees and demand reams of financial information.
- Conformity means doing *everything* in a specified way, and most franchise agreements stridently insist that business be conducted in a precise fashion. That can be hard on you if you've set out to be your own master. Any deviation, and you could be out of luck—and thousands of dollars.

As with any investment, you first need to sit down and figure out what your return is going to be. In the short term you have to get enough out of the business to live on. In the long term you want the business to appreciate in value so you can possibly sell it and enjoy a huge capital gain. Chances are you're not going to get very rich owning a Mac's Milk franchise. The odds are a lot better with a McDonald's. Of course, getting behind a Big Mac is also going to cost you a lot more initially.

When you evaluate a franchise, look at the kind of support services the company is willing to provide. You want as much help as you can get. But also investigate what the franchisor wants from you—will you be required to buy supplies just from him, or will you retain the right to shop around and get the best deal you can?

Most important, have long talks with people who are already dealing with these guys. See if they are happy, and if they're content with the profits their businesses are earning.

Most often franchise businesses are advertised in business newspapers, the financial sections of dailies and in the classifieds under "Business Opportunities." A growing trend is to have franchisors attract clients by setting up booths at money-oriented trade shows and fairs. The country's largest is held early in February in Toronto and attracts tens of thousands of people.

A book well worth picking up is the Association of Canadian Franchisors' *Franchise Annual*. It lists all the franchises available in the country, gives you contact names, address and phone numbers and spells out every company's financial requirements. The cost: $29 by mail, or $25 if you pick it up in Toronto. The address: Association of Canadian Franchisors, 88 University Avenue, Suite 607, Toronto, Ont. M5J 1T8. If you want to phone in an order, the number is (416) 595-5005.

Okay, another big decision is how you are going to carry on in business. It's not enough to hang out a sign and do it. You have to think of things like legal protection and tax implications. And what happens if you start Wombat Escort Services, it thrives, and then somebody across the street starts a business with the same name? Without some kind of legals, you can't do a thing about it.

So one of the first decisions to make is what form of business structure you will choose—a sole proprietorship, a partnership or a limited company. I have always preferred to incorporate and do business through a provincially chartered limited company.

The first one I set up, in 1975, was for my newspaper venture, and I did the legal work myself, establishing three directors and officers—myself and my two investors. Several years later Dorothy and I set up two numbered companies, through which we could conduct various affairs. One handles a mail-order and publishing business, while the other receives income from commercial real estate investments. I also incorporated both without the use of a lawyer. Doing this is pretty simple—just send away to the province for the forms (addresses are listed later in this chapter), get a book from the library or bookstore giving you the proper legal language, and then mail the package back in. It can take some time to process, especially if the name you pick happens to be in use already.

That's why numbered companies are popular—you don't have to wait for name clearance. The province simply assigns a number that is yours alone, and then you can apply for an "operating style," which is good for five years and is renewable. For example, one company I own is numbered, and it operates under the style of "Turner Associates." That means somebody can write a cheque payable to either the number or the name, and the bank will accept it.

The last company I incorporated, in 1987, was a new retail operation, and this time I used a lawyer. I also wanted name protection, which is important for a retail business. To give you an idea of costs, I paid the province $220 to make the application, $104.02 for incorporation supplies (company minute book, corporate seal, etc.) and a name search, $15 for postage, phone calls and photocopying, and $400 in legal fees. So the total cost was just under $740.

For that I received the attached articles of incorporation and a company called The Village Patriot Inc. You can see from the forms that there really was not much mystery involved in setting up this business. And now Dorothy and I have a way to do business that gives us distinct advantages. To put them in context, let's quickly run through the three legal forms of small business ownership:

- The sole proprietorship is the quick and dirty way of getting into business. It's cheap, fast and easy. All you have to do is obtain a license from the municipal government, which involves nothing more than paying a small fee.

With a sole proprietorship, you are on your own. You make all the decisions, and you take all the credit, the money and the blame. While things go well, this is great. When they don't, you're in trouble. A sole proprietorship provides no legal protection from creditors, bankers or other evil forces. If you get your business in trouble, then people you owe money to can seize your personal assets in place of business debts—that can include your bank accounts and real estate. You'll also, as a sole operator, find it a lot harder to borrow from the bank, and you will certainly be required to put up all your personal wealth as collateral for any business-related borrowing. If that makes you nervous, well, it should.

• The partnership comes in two flavors. A general partnership is made up of equals who share in the management of the small business and who also share liability for its debts. A limited partnership, on the other hand, has several partners whose liability for business debt is limited to a certain amount. But limited partners are just investors and do not take an active part in running the show. That's left to the general partners.

The essential document here is a legally binding partnership agreement, which is drawn up usually but not necessarily by a lawyer, signed by everybody involved and witnessed. Some care should be taken with the wording because disputes often (far too often) arise between partners, usually after business starts going poorly. The agreement spells out the nature of the business, the date the partnership starts and some mechanism for ending it; stipulates the operating capital, and how much each partner is chipping in; details the salaries to be paid, names the partnership's bank, describes division of profits and spells out whether this is a full- or part-time job for each partner; and includes, most importantly, a buy-out agreement. Typically, if a falling-out takes place, or one partner wants to take his money and run, then the other partners have the option to buy him out. The partnership agreement should make it clear how that's going to happen, and how a fair market price is arrived at.

A partnership obviously has some advantages. For example, you can raise more money when you have more investors. You get somebody else to help work at making the business grow. And it's pretty cheap to set up an agreement and register your partnership with the provincial government.

But, but, but. You still have unlimited liability, which means if the business goes bust your personal assets are at risk. The other big worry is that the partners will not totally agree on things and a serious dispute may arise. If it does, it's not easy or fast for partners to get out of the agreement because it takes time to assess the worth of their investment. Also, partnership does not make it any easier to go to the bank and borrow money. The banker is still going to get you to pledge personal possessions to back the loan.

• The incorporated company is really the only way I would do business. A corporation, once established, has a life of its own. It has a legal existence; it has its own name and address; it has separate records; and its debts are paid from its income and assets—not from the personal wealth of its shareholders. You incorporate either provincially or federally, depending on how widely you plan to do business. The name has to be unique, unless you use just a number. Shares are issued to the investors who are capitalizing the company.

The advantages of doing business this way are many, but the biggest is that you get limited liability. If one of my companies fell on hard times, owed the bank $400,000 and couldn't pay, it would declare bankruptcy. As a shareholder, my house, car or other holdings would be safe. All I could lose would be the money I had put into that company.

The other big advantage is that the company can earn money and keep a lot more of it than I can. The combined federal and Ontario tax rate for small businesses earning under $200,000 is just 22 percent, compared with a personal tax rate—even after tax reform—of over 40 percent. So retained earnings by a corporation are much higher.

It's also easy with an incorporated com-

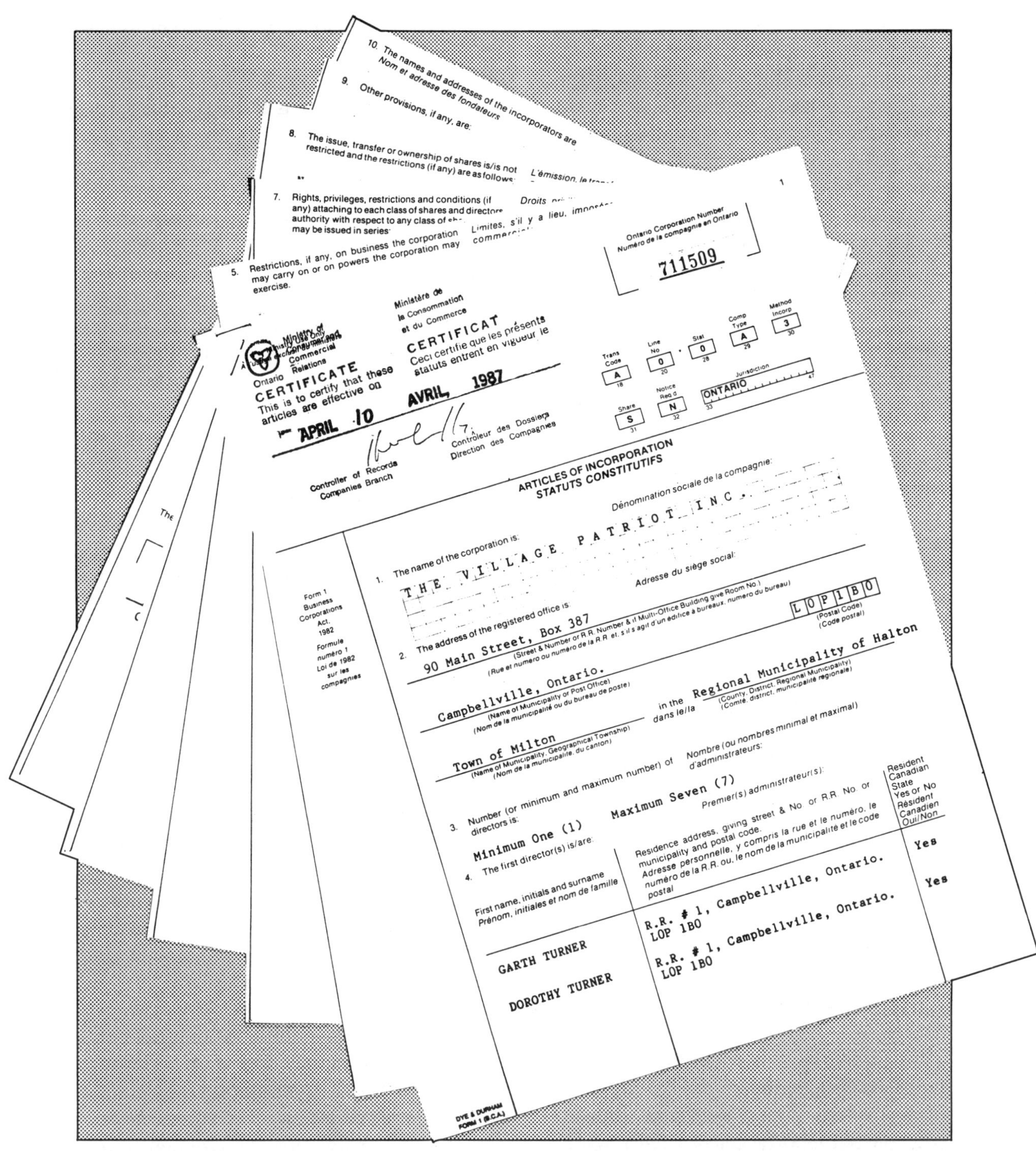

10. The names and addresses of the incorporators are
Nom et adresse des fondateurs

9. Other provisions, if any, are:

8. The issue, transfer or ownership of shares is/is not restricted and the restrictions (if any) are as follows:

7. Rights, privileges, restrictions and conditions (if any) attaching to each class of shares and directors authority with respect to any class of shares which may be issued in series:

5. Restrictions, if any, on business the corporation may carry on or on powers the corporation may exercise.

Ontario Corporation Number
Numéro de la compagnie en Ontario
711509

Ministry of Consumer and Commercial Relations
Ministère de la Consommation et du Commerce

CERTIFICATE
This is to certify that these articles are effective on
CERTIFICAT
Ceci certifie que les présents statuts entrent en vigueur le

APRIL 10 AVRIL 1987

Controller of Records Companies Branch
Contrôleur des Dossiers Direction des Compagnies

Trans Code: A | Line No: 0 | Stat: 0 | Comp Type: A | Method Incorp: 3
Share: S | Notice Req'd: N | Jurisdiction: ONTARIO

ARTICLES OF INCORPORATION
STATUTS CONSTITUTIFS

Form 1
Business Corporations Act, 1982
Formule numéro 1
Loi de 1982 sur les compagnies

1. The name of the corporation is:
Dénomination sociale de la compagnie:
THE VILLAGE PATRIOT INC.

2. The address of the registered office is:
Adresse du siège social:
90 Main Street, Box 387
(Street & Number or R.R. Number & if Multi-Office Building give Room No.)
(Rue et numéro ou numéro de la R.R. et, s'il s'agit d'un édifice à bureaux, numéro du bureau)
L0P 1B0
(Postal Code)
(Code postal)

Campbellville, Ontario.
(Name of Municipality or Post Office)
(Nom de la municipalité ou du bureau de poste)

in the / dans le/la
Regional Municipality of Halton
(County, District, Regional Municipality)
(Comté, district, municipalité régionale)

Town of Milton
(Name of Municipality, Geographical Township)
(Nom de la municipalité, du canton)

3. Number (or minimum and maximum number) of directors is:
Nombre (ou nombres minimal et maximal) d'administrateurs:
Minimum One (1) Maximum Seven (7)

4. The first director(s) is/are:
Premier(s) administrateur(s):

First name, initials and surname Prénom, initiales et nom de famille	Residence address, giving street & No. or R.R. No. or municipality and postal code. Adresse personnelle, y compris la rue et le numéro, le numéro de la R.R. ou, le nom de la municipalité et le code postal	Resident Canadian State Yes or No Résident Canadien Oui/Non
GARTH TURNER	R.R. # 1, Campbellville, Ontario. L0P 1B0	Yes
DOROTHY TURNER	R.R. # 1, Campbellville, Ontario. L0P 1B0	Yes

DYE & DURHAM FORM 1 (B.C.A.)

These are the articles of incorporation we set up in mid-1987. You can see here just how simple this procedure is. Yet having an incorporation gives you vital limited liability—you can do business without the thought of having your personal assets at risk should the venture go badly. Bankers like incorporations better than partnerships—because they're neater.

pany to raise capital by selling shares. If you get really big-time, you can turn your company into a public one, which means shares are bought and sold among investors. The board of directors (that's Dorothy and me) can vote to create more shares, and then look for other investors to buy them. And we get an easier time at the bank, as well. The company holds assets in its own name, and so can borrow against them. Of course, bankers being bankers, they will also try to get a personal guarantee and rights to your plasma—but odds are you'll do much better than with a proprietorship or partnership.

However, it does cost more money to set up a company, and it does take a longer time, although a good lawyer should be able to create a numbered company in a week and a named one in three. Also with a company you have certain obligations. You must have a complete set of banking papers, a corporate minute book and a company seal, and you will not escape taxation, because the company has a government registration and requires full annual accounting. Finally, there is a tad less privacy, because anyone can go and look through government records and see your incorporation. It is public knowledge who the directors of an incorporated company are, where they live and the location of the company's head office. So you may want to think twice about going this route if you are incorporating to carry on an illegal business.

As a last note, doing business as a corporation carries a little more weight out there in the world of suppliers, customers, lenders and so on. It shows you have taken the time to put your affairs in order and that you intend to stay in business. Nobody need know that you do business on the kitchen table, or that the corporate seal is filed next to the jar of oregano. World headquarters may be here now, but—corporately—you're ready to take on anybody.

After working with me on our first joint venture—that newspaper publishing company—Dorothy got a bit sidetracked. By conventional standards she was making great strides, but we came to feel otherwise. Five years after starting at a low-paying entry-level job with a big company, she was a senior manager, in charge of a wide range of products and managing her own corporate profit centre. At $40,000 a year, she was among the best-paid women in the organization, with a big office, personal secretary and large staff. She was on a share-purchase plan. And she was poised to take the next step up the corporate ladder.

But that didn't mean she was happy. Succeeding in a corporation means surrendering certain things. For example, the corporation wants to have first rights to your time. Offices function in a way that is supposes to encourage creativity but actually deadens it by enforcing conformity. So Dorothy had to wear power suits, arrive on time and closely adhere to a chain of command. This was not consistent with other aspects of her life, like choosing to live with me in the country, or to work on the publishing company we were building in our spare time. There was too much time being spent on getting to, succeeding at and worrying about work, relative to the return the company was willing to afford her.

Dorothy really wanted to be her own boss again, but she didn't have the courage to leave what everyone told her was a first-class position. Then I lent her a copy of psychologist Beverly Potter's new book, *The Way of the Ronin*. It was about following a centuries-old Japanese model, fashioning yourself after a special kind of samurai warrior. The ronin had left the service of the feudal warlord and lived by his wits. Potter told how Baby Boom achievers could follow a similar path to success—away from the traditional ladder-climbing and toward diversification instead of specialization. Potter was outlining a new strategy for the Corporate Ronin.

Dorothy could not put the book down. For a week she did nothing but quote paragraphs to me, and now, almost four years later, she still keeps this volume on a shelf beside her desk. For her, the way of the ronin meant once again taking control of events. It meant investing in her, rather than renting her time. It gave her the strength to reassess, to realize that what she was uncomfortable with was not working hard, but working in such a linear environment. Her corporation—like almost any big corporation—was just too narrow. The last thing it wanted was an entrepreneur in its midst.

These are some of the lines Dorothy underscored:

"Where does today's job lead? What opportunities does it open? Remember, look sideways, not always up. Climbing the ladder is not the only path.

"This is your work, your life. Think of yourself as your own boss. If you have a full-time position, think of yourself as a private contractor, a vendor, or a consultant with a long-term contract."

Also: "Some who are locked into mortgage payments, credit cards and the kids' college bills, would like to reach for self-realization but believe they cannot. Others, not willing to give up affluence, attempt to realize themselves with hobbies or volunteer work, part-time around the edges of their jobs. They are finding that they cannot actualize their self-realization goals at work after all. They are not free. The linear career is a master who permits little deviation from a straight line. These people become trapped in career feudalism."

Dorothy's immediate superior, a linear-oriented guy, would stick his feet up on his desk during business meetings with her. If anything made her break the ties, I think it was sitting there looking at the soles of his shoes. She was not free. That was the message in his body language.

Once Dorothy made the decision to leave, and we managed our own affairs, things began to improve dramatically. We are not a two-income household any longer. We are a seven-income one, with several companies, several products and diverse investments. Dorothy has more work than ever, three part-time employees and a whole range of business contacts. Instead of going to the same place every day, seeing the same faces and performing the same tasks, she may go from buying stock for the retail store to dealing with tenants or writing a print advertising campaign or researching a prospective real estate deal or bidding in an antique auction or making a bank deposit.

Meanwhile, the corporation has closed up behind her. The wound was immediately healed, and office life went on without missing a beat. It's always like that. No individual is allowed to become so important in a big company that losing them will hurt business.

She underlined this, too: "The linear career strategy was a winner in the postwar growth era, the heyday of industrialism. But as we specialized, we became, without realizing it, interchangeable, standardized parts in the industrial machine, the organization. Jobs were defined, classified, standardized. Just as an auto mechanic can order new plugs when the old ones misfire or replace worn wheel bearings, the organization can replace specialized workers."

This is what those who become entrepreneurs come to realize. There is no longer job security in this economy. After Black Monday the layoffs that started in the financial sector and quickly spread were reminders that corporations exist to survive, not to reward employees. Security lies only in the hands of those who control their own enterprise. This is what small business is all about. It means setting your own agenda, and you can't start too soon.

Who is most likely to succeed as an entrepreneur? According to Ontario's 1987 report on small business, 81 percent of successful small business owners held previous jobs as executives or managers. Only 7 percent had held professional jobs, and just 5 percent had been in sales. It's interesting to note that while 21 percent of small businesses had been started by people who were skilled in the trades, only 1 percent of successful companies had been. Obviously the success rate is low for them and high for people with management experience.

Why do small businesses fail? For lots of reasons, and typically within the first five years of life. The statistics are disheartening. Half of all new businesses fail in the first year, and a staggering 90 percent pass away within five. Almost all the failures can be attributed to the entrepreneur's incompetence—inexperience at managing a certain kind of business or in handling finances. Most often those in trouble mask their problems by blaming their failure on outside forces.

The excuse I hear most often is, "The bank won't give me enough money." Some people are naive enough to think banks routinely provide close to 100 percent financing for start-up operations. The reality is that a new entrepreneur is lucky if a bank will match his or her personal investment, and an operating line of credit comes only after the business proves it can establish a good cash flow.

Other reasons why businesses fail often involve money—not enough invested at the outset, an inability to finance expansion, a lack of working capital or an inability to get credit from suppliers. You also have to make sure your product or service is right for the market; your costs are kept strictly in line; your location is right; your expansion is moderate and well-planned; and your marketing is effective in cost and reach. If people don't know you're in business, chances are you won't be for long. Self-promotion is crucial to survival.

Getting into business is no picnic. Buying a franchise or an existing operation reduces the risk factor considerably.. Make sure you link your fervor to succeed with proper advice. Get a lawyer and get an accountant. You'll need them to set up a company, purchase a business or franchise, assess financial statements and look for early danger signs. Don't try to cheap your way out by cutting these corners. I have learned through experience that it is not a wise thing to do. It can, in fact, be deadly.

There is no reason why you have to go into this alone. Lots of help is available. For example:

- The Canadian Federation of Independent Business, John Bulloch's outfit, has reams of support material and statistical data that is helpful to the first-time entrepreneur. Members receive newsletters, surveys and studies, while Bulloch lobbies in Ottawa. Suite 401, 4141 Yonge Street, Willowdale, Ont. M2P 2A6
- The Canadian Organization of Small

Business is a much smaller but spirited group originally formed by splinter elements of the Canadian Federation of Independent Business. Also providers of helpful info. Suite 310, 7050 Woodbine Avenue, Markham, Ont. L3R 4G8.

- The Entrepreneurship Institute of Canada is worth writing to. It's backed by several major corporations and was set up to encourage people like you who are considering setting out on their own. 256 Columbia Street W., Waterloo, Ont. N2L 3L3.
- The Federal Business Development Bank has offices across Canada. This federal agency was set up to help encourage small business creation. It offers loans, but don't look for any deals better than the banks'. The best service is a counselling one, often staffed by retired businessmen and executives who can put their experience where their mouths are.
- The Small Business Secretariat is part of the federal Department of Regional Industrial Expansion. Yeah, more bureaucrats, but they do have some useful information contained in free booklets on small biz. There are provincial offices across Canada, with the headquarters at: 235 Queen Street, Ottawa, Ont. K1A 0H5.

Also, every province also has agencies set up to assist small corporations, and they offer a rainbow of services. Never forget that provinces regularly pour a ton of money into the private sector so politicians can stand up in the legislature and brag about how many jobs their governments have created. If they're dishing it out, you might as well take some. Here, by province, is where to write for a package of services offered:

- British Columbia: Ministry of Industry and Small Business, 1045 Douglas Street, Victoria, B.C. V8W 3C1.
- Alberta: Ministry of Tourism and Small Business, 10025 Jasper Avenue, Edmonton , Alta. T5J 3Z3.
- Saskatchewan: Department of Tourism and Small Business, Bank of Montreal Bldg., 2103 11th Avenue, Regina, Sask. S4P 3V7.
- Manitoba: Manitoba Business Development and Tourism, 155 Carlton Street, Winnipeg, Man. R3C 3H8.
- Ontario: Ministry of Industry, Trade and Technology Small Business Branch, 900 Bay Street, Toronto, Ont. M7A 2E4.
- Quebec: Industrial Development Corporation, Suite 700, 1125 Chemin Saint-Louis, Sillery, Que. G1S 1E5.
- New Brunswick: Department of Commerce and Development, Small Business Division, Box 6000, Fredericton, N.B. E3B 5H1.
- Nova Scotia: Department of Development, World Trade and Convention Centre, 1800 Argyle Street, Box 519, Halifax, N.S. B3J 2R7.
- Prince Edward Island: Department of Industry, Industrial Development Division, Box 2000, Charlottetown, P.E.I. C1A 7N8.
- Newfoundland: Department of Development and Tourism, Box 4750, St. John's, Nfld. A1C 5T7.

Finally, I think it might be a good idea if you went out and spent some money on some other books. There are a raft of them on small business and the entrepreneurial spirit. A lot of them say the same things and many are useless because the're American. Others, however, are worthwhile and may end up answering a lot of questions as well as helping you to avoid mistakes.

This list is by no means exhaustive, but these are some of the titles from my own library:

- *Start and Run Your Own Successful*

Business, by Peter Cook. This is called "an entrepreneur's guide" and is written by a chartered accountant. It's not a bad book, but look to it more for general trends and opinion than for a lot of how-to stuff. (General Publishing, $16.95.)

- *Financial Control for the Small Business,* by Michael Coltman, is also written by an accountant, and it's useful for one thing: it teaches you to interpret a balance sheet. The author says it's so business operators can spot coming trouble, but it's also a good skill for those studying the numbers of a prospective business venture. Cheap, too. (International Self-Counsel Press, $5.50.)
- *Own Your Own Franchise,* by Ray Bard and Sheila Henderson, is an American book, but I include it because it's over four hundred pages detail what franchises are available, what they cost, what the companies do and their business track record. A great number of the franchises examined are available in Canada. (Addison Wesley, $20.95.)
- *The Entrepreneur's Complete Self-Assessment Guide,* by Doug Gray, contains tests to determine if you, cookie, have the stuff it takes to go it on your own. Also some workbook-type stuff on financing, incorporating and putting together a business plan. Written by a lawyer/consultant, it's not a bad buy. (International Self-Counsel Press, $9.95)
- *Starting and Managing Your Own Small Business* by Maurice Archer and Jerry White, was published in the late 1970s, but it's still a useful reference book. It contains a great deal of information on how to set up a business and then keep it healthy. Published jointly by the *Financial Post* and Macmillan of Canada, it was the first book in the Canadian Small Business Series. Look for this one in your public library.
- *Money Makers!* should be read for inspiration and good product/marketing ideas. It profiles about forty Canadian success stories, some of them small and some huge. An offshoot of Global TV's "Everybody's Business" show, it was compiled by host Everett Banning and producer Kenneth Barnes. (McClelland and Steward, $24.95.)
- *Small Business Management Fundamentals,* by Andrew Szonyi and Dan Steinhoff, was published as a textbook ten years ago, and sold then for $14.50. This exhaustive look at small business contains a ton of information; it's been updated and is still in use. Worth finding a copy through the College Division of McGraw-Hill Ryerson.
- *The State of Small Business* is the annual report of the Ontario Committee of Parliamentary Assistants for Small Business, and it's not as boring as you might think. Inside is a lot of interesting info on what kinds of business are being created and by what type of people. You can get it from the Ontario Government Bookstore, 880 Bay Street., Toronto M7A 1N8, for just five bucks. Or you can call Ontario's Small Business Hotline at 1-800-387-6142.
- *Women Mean Business,* by Moneca Litton, is aimed at (what else?) women who are thinking about starting a business. The author goes through the usual stuff about being an entrepreneur, marketing, forms of business and financing. I don't think advice to women should be any different than to men, but if dividing the world by sex is your bag, this is the latest entry. (Key Porter,$16.95.)
- *The Way of the Ronin,* by Beverly Potter, has to be on this list, or Dorothy would give me a hard time. It's all about how to stop being an employee and to start being self-driven, living a diversified life. It works. I've witnessed it. (Prentice-Hall Canada, $24.95.)

Chapter 5

So, where is money safe

Where is money safe? That's a big question, and throughout this book we've been sneaking up on it. I've talked about cash investments like Treasury bills and savings bonds and mortgage-backed securities, about metals like gold and silver, about the stock market and the security of real estate. But everything keeps changing, and fluctuations in the economy mean assets perform in different ways.

As I write this in early 1988, for example, the price of gold bullion has crashed below the $450 U.S./oz. mark, its worst showing in more than a year. It fell $13 in a day, and $15 over a weekend. Why? And does this mean it's a good time to buy?

Gold prices took a big drop for two main reasons. First, U.S. leading economic indicators have taken a drop, which means there is probably a recession coming. (I think it's inevitable.) If the States goes into recession, the economy would, of course, slow down. Individual Americans would spend less money, and imports would slow. That would in turn help the U.S. trade deficit, and so the American dollar would rise. Gold, which is priced in those dollars, would consequently fall. So, the expectation that a recession may begin in the months ahead has caused gold to drop.

But that's just part of the reason. A few days ago there was a report out of Finland that the Soviet Union had suffered another nuclear power plant accident. Moscow denied the report, but gold suffered anyway, because after the Chernobyl disaster the U.S.S.R. had to sell off a lot of gold (the country is a huge producer) to finance the clean-up, which cost over a billion rubles, or roughly $8 billion U.S. Whenever a big amount of gold comes on the market, supply overwhelms demand and the price drops. Even the expectation of a lot of gold to come can have the same effect.

So recession and nuclear worries have just hit gold hard, but conditions will be different when you read this page. The point here is that investment conditions can change overnight. If you need more proof, leaf back to the chapter on Black Monday. I remember watching "Wall Street Week" on Friday, October 16. The show's experts were telling investors not to worry about the day's 100-point drop on the Dow Jones index. The bull market is still intact, they said. Three days later the index plunged 508 points.

Nothing cataclysmic had happened, and yet things just went straight to hell. In the wake of that, the economy has been put at risk because people are psychologically bruised. So, more than ever, you need to be cautious about your wealth. You need to play it safe if you want to survive.

And, by the way, you ask, is gold a good buy below $450 U.S. an ounce? I think it is. In the months ahead it may well go lower—possibly, quite a bit lower—but the 1990s will bring us a period of major economic expansion, likely accompanied by high

INTERNATIONAL GOLD PRICES

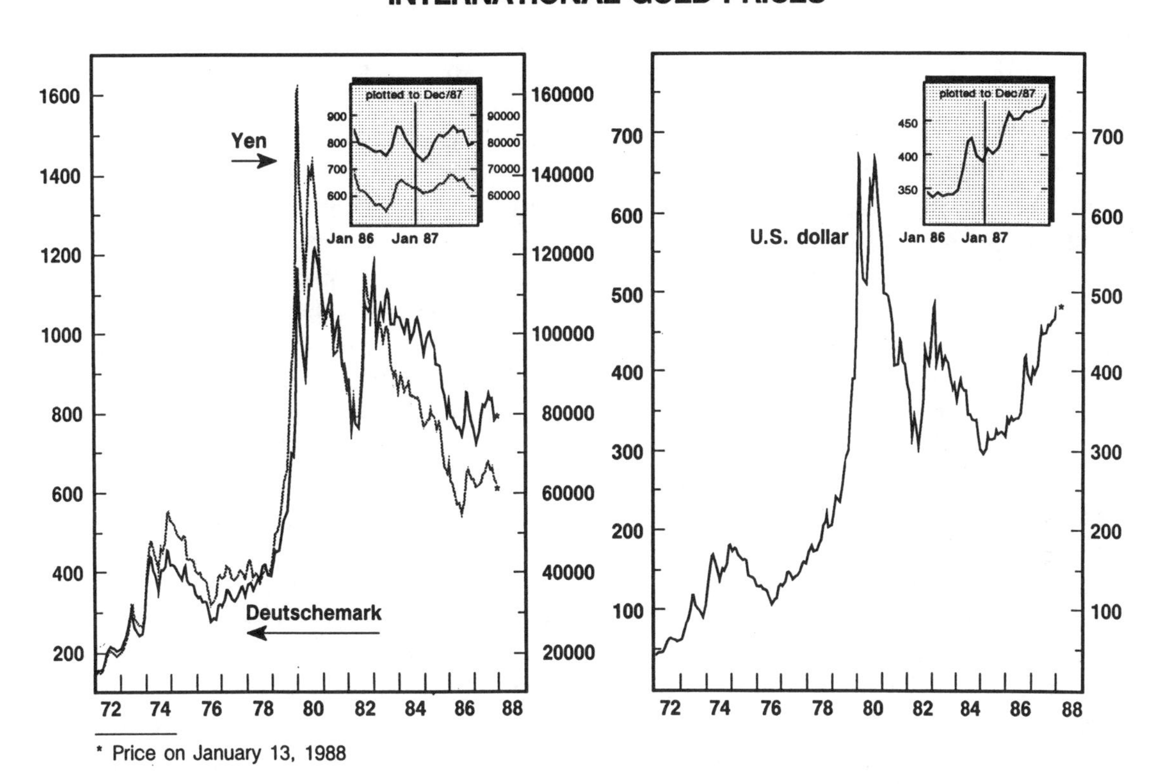

The price of a commodity depends very much on what currency you're buying it with. These two charts, prepared by Scotiabank, show the price of gold in Japanese yen, West German marks and Yankee dollars. While gold values trended steadily higher for Americans, they were drifting lower for the Germans and the Japanese, representing great value. You can see that gold prices are still far off their 1980 highs. Since this chart was drawn, gold prices have softened considerably in a way that most analysts interpret as preceding a recession.

inflation. We are coming off an expansionary high now, going into a period of sometimes-depressing adjustment, and will come out of it into a new superboom. At that time gold will rocket in value as paper money inflates, but its gains will be overshadowed by that of silver. More on this shortly.

First, let's stand back a minute and look at The Big Picture. Let's see how various investments have performed over the past fory-odd years. The following chart, prepared by American financial experts John Dorfman and Karin DeVenuta, tracks the performance of different assets since World War Two.

You can see what likes recession (stocks and bonds), what likes boom times (real estate), what likes inflation (commodities and metals) and what likes stable prices (stocks). This is important to remember, especially now as we stand on the threshold of potentially rotten times. When recession materializes you would be smart to have your wealth close at hand in cash or cashable assets, ready to invest in bargain stocks (if you've got the stomach for it) and income-producing real estate. As the recession ends, cash out of the stock market and go heavily into precious metals and other commodities.

But how do you know when these big cycles in the economy are dawning or retreating? You stay informed, that's how. Read newspapers and current-affairs magazines, find commentators you believe in, watch trends and generally work at collecting new knowledge. The day you stop, expertise degenerates into luck.

There are four little rules I would like to toss in at this point:

1) **Be liquid**. Liquid assets are the ones you can turn into cash fast, like savings bonds, Treasury bills, or investment assets like mutual funds, stocks, RRSPS and precious metals. Non-liquid assets are things like real estate, art or antiques—buyers are not necessarily found immediately. No, I'm not telling you to abandon real estate, because this is one of the safest, surest investments around. As mentioned earlier, you should have a principal residence, and this should be the cornerstone of your financial plan. And, yes, income-producing properties are great, but all your wealth should not be tied up in non-liquid stuff, especially with poor economic times looming. Right now liquidity is important. Times are changing quickly, and you need the ability to roll with the punches.

2) **Diversify**. Don't put your eggs in one basket unless you are very sure of what you're doing. There are lots of ways that you can invest, and by spreading your wealth around you minimize your exposure to changes in the economy. One of the worst things you can do is go deeply in debt, for example by mortgaging a big principal residence and then depending on cash flow to service that debt. The house earns you nothing while it costs you greatly in after-tax dollars. This impairs your ability to diversify and puts you at risk in case a recession cuts off some of your family income. Too many people have walked into this potential trap during the past twenty months. Instead of moving up in the housing market, they should have been spreading their savings around, getting into income-producing investments—diversifying. When the lesson hits, it will hit hard.

3) **Don't exceed your personal level of risk.** Investments can be very safe or they

Average Annual Return on Investment
(in percent)

Investment	Recession	Boom	High Inflation	Low Inflation
Bonds (long-term gov't)	17	4	-1	8
Commodity Index	1	-6	15	-5
Diamonds	-4	8	79	15
Gold	-8	-9	105	19
Private home	4	6	6	5
Real estate (commercial)	9	13	18	6
Silver	3	-6	94	4
Stocks (blue chip)	14	7	3	21
Treasury bills	6	5	7	3

can be extremely risky. Putting money into a term deposit, guaranteed investment certificate, Treasury bill, mortgage-backed security or savings bond is 100 percent free of risk. Investing in mortgage-based mutual funds is also quite safe. Putting money into funds based on stocks or currencies is not. The stock market is volatile. Trading in options and futures is laden with risk. Precious metals are currently very dangerous.

In return for minimizing your risk, you'll have to be content with a yield of 10 percent or less, which is not too shabby when you consider early 1988's inflation rate of less than 5 percent. The higher the rate of return you want, the more risk you'll have to take. Equity-based mutual funds in 1987, for example, were returning 15 percent to 20 percent, but then look what happened in October. The value of many funds fell by 30 percent, and, as a result, Canadians scrambled to withdraw over $2 billion. And gold rose steadily from the $320 range in early 1986 to $400 as 1987 opened, right through to $500 in December. But prices have dumped since, and the future is unclear. You can gamble if you want—and sometimes it's a lot of fun. Just recognize what you are doing, and establish early how much pain you can endure.

4) The best investment on earth is in debt. Nothing is more important in days like these than paying down the money you owe. Only in a time of wild, double-digit inflation, when the value of paper money is falling fast, does it make sense to accumulate debt. As the 1980s come to an end, the value of paper money increases, and that makes debt harder to service. Real disposable incomes have been dropping, wage gains are small and cash is harder to come by. Meanwhile taxes have sharply increased, as the government also tries to cope with debt. In an environment like this, it is crazy to be carrying a lot of credit. Right now it is much easier to save money than to earn it, and it makes more sense to take your savings and reduce debt than it does to invest them.

For example, if you earn 10 percent on a cash investment, you are fully taxed on that income, including the inflation component of 5 percent. That reduces your real, after-tax return to no more than 3 percent. Meanwhile a mortgage at 10 percent is payable in dollars that have already been taxed, and so for most middle-class people that raises its effective rate to almost 14 percent. Doesn't it make more sense to pay off the mortgage than it does to have a cash investment? You bet it does.

Speaking of debt, there is smart debt and the stupid kind. Borrowing smart is on a credit card that you pay off each month. Borrowing smart is with an interest-only demand loan when interest rates are falling. Borrowing smart is a fixed-rate, long-term mortgage when rates are on the way up. And borrowing smart at any time is a mortgage with weekly-pay, annual prepayments or increased monthly-pay options.

Borrowing stupid is a conventional mortgage with monthly payments and amortized over twenty-five years. That way you end up paying the bank about three times what you borrowed. Borrowing stupid is running a balance at 16 percent or better on credit cards. Really borrowing stupid is using a card from a department store or oil company—those bandits still rob people at the rate of 28 percent.

Borrowing stupid also includes getting involved with one of those homeowner's lines of credit that started to hit the market in a big way in 1987. For a few years now, banks and trust companies have been pushing personal lines of credit—you can have access to funds by simply writing a personal cheque. It means the end to interviews with the loans officer every time you want to borrow. You simply arrange a line of credit, and then you're covered when your account falls into overdraft. The convenience is large, and so is the interest charged, because a line of credit is not really secured by anything physical.

The homeowner line of credit is a refinement of that, and while it may be appealing, it comes with dangers attached. The benefit is that at a place like the Bank of Montreal, you can borrow as much as $150,000 just by whipping out your cheque book. That would allow you to do a major renovation, for example, or invest the money in something else for a better return. The rate charged is reasonable—a half-point below the prime, and you only have to repay 2 percent of the outstanding balance, or $100, whichever is greater in a month.

The bank will loan you up to 70 percent of the appraised value of your real estate, give you a monthly statement and life-insure your loan. That all sounds good, but this line of credit (not just at the Bank of Montreal but also at Canada Trust and others) comes with something sinister behind it—a mortgage.

The bank can give you so much money and at such a reasonable rate because the line of credit is secured by a collateral mortgage on your house. Arranged at your own expense, it requires you to have an appraisal done and to hire a lawyer. The cost is typically be between $400 and $600. Worse, should you not be able to repay the money you've borrowed when the bank wants it, your real estate could be seized under a power of sale and sold off to pay your debts. Effectively, you've let the bank place a second mortgage on your house. And because the line of credit is at a variable interest rate—it moves up and down with the prime—you are also fully exposed to rate increases.

What all this means is that there are a lot better places to go for money, like a personal termplan loan with a fixed interest rate and a set payment schedule. (By the way, most people don't realize it, but loan rates are flexible. Loans officers usually have the authority to drop the cost of a loan, and banks are fiercely competitive to get this kind of business. There's no reason to accept the first rate you're quoted. Tell the bank you want a loan at prime. If you end up getting it for prime plus one or one and a half, you'll have done well.)

Here's the first rule of borrowing: Always make sure you borrow for a good reason. Remember, the first thing you do is pay down your debt. Also make sure you're living within your means. If you borrow, try to make the interest tax-deductible. That happens with an investment loan used to buy an asset that will produce income.

Borrow only to buy things that appreciate in value—like real estate. Do not borrow to buy stuff you know will depreciate—like cars. Rent or lease depreciating assets; buy appreciating ones. If you remember nothing else, remember that.

Canadians can be excused for making some wrong investment decisions. It often happens because of a simple lack of information. But it also happens because gutless provincial regulators have allowed the financial planning industry to remain unregulated, unsupervised and largely undisciplined. Sure, there are some good planners, but for every honest and conscientious one there are a dozen more who are nothing but salespeople in the cloak of planners. Most Canadian financial planners are practicing misrepresentation and deceit.

Stockbrokers need a license to work; so do insurance agents and mechanics. Personal financial planners do not. You don't need any credentials to call yourself a financial advisor or personal financial planner. None. Consider Boris "Bo" Regaard, certified in 1985 as a financial planner and a member of the International Association of Financial Planners. Bo Regaard is a Tampa, Florida, poodle. His owner, himself a financial planner, registered the mutt to show that the association, the title and the nice certificate didn't mean squat.

Because these people aren't licenced, catalogued or registered, nobody even knows how many there are. One thing that's become clear, though, is that their numbers are multiplying. So where can you go for real financial planning advice? What are the kinds of planners to watch out for?

The big problem is finding an advisor who isn't more interested in selling you something than helping you decide what to do. These salespeople account for probably 80 percent of all the personal financial planners in Canada. They are mostly insurance agents, mutual fund salespeople and account reps for stock brokerage houses, who portray themselves as impartial advisors. Open the newspaper, especially during RRSP season, and you can see the ads for "financial planners" who are giving free seminars on successful investing. Also note that these events are sponsored by companies that sell financial products, usually mutual funds.

And don't be fooled by the designation "certified financial planner" or be impressed that someone is a member of a trade association of planners. About 90 percent of the membership is people who work on commission—companies pay them to sell things to people who come and ask for advice. It is ridiculously easy to gain membership in these associations, and no federal or provincial guidelines are in place to regulate their conduct.

If you are shopping for an advisor, make sure you ask the right questions:

- Find out how long the company's been operating and who it is affiliated with—that is, what financial products does it represent?
- Ask how the planner is going to be paid. If he tells you not to worry because the advice is free, go someplace else. Better to find somebody paid by fee—by you—than by commission by somebody else. Typically, a fee-for-service advisor may cost you $100 an hour, and some charge as much as $5,000 for a complete action plan with an annual review.
- Ask what the advisor's qualifications are. Being a "certified financial planner" just isn't good enough. The advisor should have some tax, accounting or law training. Ask to see some of his work, including past plans. Ask for a brief (half-hour) session in which he or she can get a general sense of your financial status and make some general suggestions. Get a feel for the advisor's competence.
- Ask for references. Ask if this advisor can recommend other people to carry out the financial plan he'll design for you. And ask about follow-up help, because changing tax laws and markets mean you'll need help.

Don't just throw your life into someone else's hands. I've seen a lot of people do that—usually dentists, for some strange reason—and the consequences can be tragic, especially where an investment was made simply to save on taxes. You should seek help and ask for the information you need to *understand* the investments you're making.

Don't be talked into borrowing against the equity in your home to buy into a mutual fund, especially if you are retired and the house is paid for. Sleaze "planners" commonly try to pull this off, picking up a 9 percent commission. Don't put money into a savings plan, even if this results in a tax saving, until your debt situation is under control. Remain cautious about the stock market, because it is extremely volatile and may reach new lows. Many mutual funds are based on stock values, so make sure you understand what you're buying. Most people who ask me for help have no idea what the funds they've bought really are.

It's also a good idea to never go with a single opinion. Bounce the same questions off your broker, accountant and bank manager; then compare answers and make your own decisions. Often people who think they need advisors and a financial plan require nothing more than some common sense. It's easier to save money than to make it. It's better to be a lender than a borrower. You can't live beyond your means for very long. There's no free lunch.

When you start thinking about your financial plan, decide what your personal objectives will be. Do you want to shelter your wealth, build up more or just ensure security? A lot will depend on how old you are, your family commitments and your personal lifestyle.

Investments can pay you back in one of two ways: through income or in the form of a capital gain. We've looked at income-producers, like guaranteed investment certificates, savings bonds and Cannie Maes. Dividend-paying stocks also produce income. So does investment real estate.

A capital gain is the profit you make from buying an asset low and selling it high. This could be a piece of land or a wafer of gold or a stock that has risen in value. The capital gain profit comes after you deduct the money it cost you to carry the asset while you owned it. Investments that produce income also produce taxes all the time that income flows into your hands. Investments that produce capital gains do not produce taxes until you come to realize that gain—and then you can get a break.

The profit you make by selling your principal residence is tax-free. This Canadian tradition compensates us for not getting a tax break on mortgage interest as the Americans do. In addition, a $100,000 lifetime capital gains tax exemption is still in place for capital gains on other investments. For how long is anybody's guess, because the move is on to tax capital gains more heavily. Still, while it's there it makes a lot of sense to use it.

I've touched on precious metals—about gold as an alternative currency and how these metals perform in times of inflation or recession. Gold, silver, platinum and palladium pay no interest, and the only way you're going to make money is if they rise in price, yielding you a capital gain. Gold hit a peak of $800 U.S. an ounce in 1980 and then sank below $300. It recovered in late 1987 to $500 and now, early in 1988, it's again in trouble. I believe gold will have another big break-out with a real collapse of the American dollar, a global market crash, a banking crisis or a bout of serious inflation. I regret to inform you that all of the above are possible.

Despite its wild fluctuations, though, I

like gold. I have several gold investments, and I can tell you that holding a 10-ounce wafer in your hand is an experience you won't forget. The metal, unlike paper money, has an intrinsic value. It is universally recognized. It is portable and eternal. Unlike paper money, it has history on its side. But it is also volatile and not for everybody. The best way to buy gold is on a regular basis, a little bit each week or month. That way you can even out price swings and establish a saner average cost. If you're in a big city, or willing to visit one, gold is easy to buy.

Money put into gold becomes more or less invisible, leaving the system and disappearing from the eyes of tax cops. For that reason, take some care in how you buy the metal. Do it at the right place and in the right way. Gold purchased for cash and taken away in physical form is best. Walk in with either U.S. or Canadian dollars, get the gold, then put it in a secure place. That could be a safety deposit box, but remember that gold is a good currency in times of economic or political upheaval—which means you might need it (and probably would) when the banks weren't open.

Two excellent gold merchants are Deak Perera and Guardian Trust. Gold bought from them for cash will come free of any paperwork identifying you as the buyer or specifying your social insurance number. You can also buy bullion through banks, especially the Royal and Scotiabank, but these guys insist on leaving a trail of paper behind them. Their gold tends to be a little more expensive, and it often takes longer to get delivery—especially at outlying branches. Bank gold may also come with the institution's logo stamped on it—which makes the metal less attractive to another dealer.

Buy gold in wafers. One-ounce to 10-ounce are best, because part of your holdings can be liquidated at any given time. The disadvantage of a larger size, such as a 100-ounce bar, is that it can't be partially sold. The advantage is that bar charges drop as the hunk of gold gets bigger.

You can also buy gold (or silver) in the form of certificates, which means the gold merchant holds the metal for you and you get a piece of paper saying you own it. This gives some people more freedom of mind, but it seems to run counter to the basic idea of gold ownership—liquid, portable, storm-proofed wealth.

Peter Cavelti is Canada's chief gold guru, and you can learn a lot more about all this by reading one of his two books. *How to Invest in Gold* is a good 180-page primer; *Gold, Silver and Strategic Metals* is more in-depth. Both are widely available in bookstores.

And finally, stay away from exotic metals, like platinum. A lot of other factors move the price of this metal. For example, it is widely used in the manufacture of catalytic converters for cars—pollution-control devices—and the auto sector is going into a steep cyclical decline. Industrial demand for platinum is expected to decline significantly just as major new sources of supply come on-line, especially from South Africa.

If you want to become a gold investor, it helps to understand the language. This glossary of common terms comes from the Gold Information Center. They'd be happy to send you a package on gold investing. Just write: 900 Third Avenue, New York, NY, 10022 U.S.A.

- Alloy: A mixture of metals. Gold, an extremely soft metal, is often alloyed with small amounts of copper, nickel, silver or zinc to make it harder. This is the case with the popular U.S. Eagle coin, which is 3 percent copper. The Canadian Maple Leaf is purer.

- Arbitrage: The act of simultaneously buying and selling a commodity (or a stock) in different markets to take advantage of price differences.
- Assay: To test a metal for its purity.
- Bid/Ask: Bid is the price a dealer will pay for gold bullion coins, and ask is the selling price offered by the dealer.
- Bullion: Gold in the form of bars, wafers or ingots. Most bars are of .995 purity or finer, which is 99.5 percent pure gold.
- Bullion coin: A minted gold coin held for investment, like the Maple Leaf, U.S. Eagle or South African Krugerrand.
- Cash price (also called spot price): The price required for immediate settlement, since most gold transactions are in cash.
- Electrolytic gold: The electric refining of gold, which produces gold of .999 fineness.
- Fine gold: Another term for pure gold.
- Fineness: The quantity of gold contained in 1000 parts of an alloy. A .995 bar contains 995 parts gold and 5 parts alloy.
- Fine weight: The pure gold weight of a bar or coin.
- Fixings: Each day in London the price is fixed twice, once at 10 am and again at 3 pm, by members of the London Gold Market. Five major traders agree on a price at which they can settle transactions.
- Four nines: Gold with a fineness of .9999, the finest gold available. Experts call it "four nines of fine gold."
- Futures contract: A contract between a buyer and seller of a commodity or security, agreeing to pay a certain price at a specified date.
- Gold standard: A monetary system based on convertibility into gold. Paper money is then backed by gold and is interchangeable with it. A country can't issue more currency than the value of the gold it owns. The U.S. went off the gold standard in 1971—the birth of inflation.
- Hallmark: The stamp on the gold bar or wafer, indicating the refiner and the fineness.
- Karat: A unit of fineness equal to 1/24 part of gold in an alloy. So, 24 carat is pure gold. The U.S. Eagle gold coin is 22 carat.

Karat gold: Gold of not less than 10 karat fineness.

- Kilo bar: A bar weighing one kilogram, or about 32.15 ounces. A total joy to hold.
- Liquid gold: A solution of gold and chemicals used for surface decoration.
- London delivery bar: A gold bar of approximately 400 troy ounces, with a minimum fineness of .995, and carrying the markings of a melter or assayer. It is the trading unit used in the London Gold Market.
- Nugget: Gold washed from rock and usually deposited in riverbeds. The largest nugget on record, found in Australia in 1972, weighed almost 200 pounds.
- Numismatic coins: Coins, metals and medallions prized as collectibles because of their rarity. They are not legal tender and can't be bought or sold as bullion pieces, so there is no guarantee of a two-way market. Generally, premiums for numismatic coins are higher than for bullion coins.
- Premium: The amount by which the selling price of a gold coin exceeds the spot value of its gold content. Part of the premium is repaid when you sell the coin. The Eagle, for example, was selling at a premium of $48 U.S. when it first went on sale.
- Short: In futures terminology going short

means to sell a commodity you do not yet possess.
- Stop loss: The placement of a buying or selling order against an existing futures contract, designed to limit your potential loss.
- Straddle: A futures trading term. A trader may sell July gold and purchase an identical amount of November gold to exploit a price difference. Also called a spread.
- Troy ounce: A unit of weight for precious metals. One troy ounce equals 1.09711 ounces, or 31.103 grams.
- Wafer: Bullion manufactured in a flat rectangle. Wafers come in various weights, up to a kilo bar.

The road to financial independence is different for everyone. It twists and turns depending on the degree of risk you're comfortable with, your determination to get ahead and how well you're able to anticipate where the economy's going. No longer can people afford to ignore the Bank of Canada rate, the deficit, the value of the dollar or the inflation rate. Our political leaders have let Canada get so indebted that we're going to flap with every economic breeze that blows by. What happens in America is going to have more impact here than at any time in our history. And America is staring deep trouble dead in the eye.

But that doesn't mean you can't make it any more. In fact, the kind of wild boom-and-bust cycles we've seen take over in the 1980s bring with them their own special opportunities. Look, for example, at the real estate market—in the dumps from 1982 to 1984 in most major markets, and then outperforming everything else three years later. Smart investors were out buying when everyone else was quivering. And they made a killing.

Or how about the stock market—from bust to boom to bust over the course of five years. Once the current market nears bottom, there are going to be some stunning buying opportunities. Then there's gold, from $800 an ounce to $400, back to $500 and headed down again. The experts agree that the metal will again test its one-time highs. It's just a matter of timing.

There is one thing absolutely clear in my mind: if you do nothing, you're going to fail. Count on it. Just lie there and let life roll over you, expecting the feds to feed you when you're old, and you'll die bitter and disillusioned. The cupboard is bare, and survival lies right in those two hands of yours. Do what I suggested: determine your net worth and then set out to make that bottom line grow.

You can do this in several ways. The most important is to actively manage your investments, getting the biggest bang for your buck and taking the time to learn about the alternatives. There is no reason why you should have more than grocery money in your savings account. Make your money earn a higher rate of return with a tiered bank account, term deposit, GIC or T-bill. Tiered accounts are now common at most banks and pay more interest as the size of the deposit grows. Some don't pay top bucks until $75,000 is invested. Give me that and I'll buy you three income properties!

As I have been telling you, it's easier to save than to earn, so have a hard look at your lifestyle and start putting aside more of your cash flow for investment. Don't be afraid to take the first step, either. I remember agonizing with Dorothy over going to the bank the first time, to ask for $200,000 in bridge financing to pull off a real estate deal. In hindsight I have no idea why we felt like that. The deal made sense. It would put us in a positive cash flow. It was a property we wanted. The price was fair. It has rocketed in value since. The downside risk was very slight—and yet we stayed up all night worrying about it. Then I realized that here was a bank willing to hand me $200,000, to secure a valuable asset. I'd pay interest only (no principal) on the loan and the bank would charge me only $54.79 a day. Fifty-four bucks? How could I lose?

Since taking that first step, each successive one has been easier. Some days I feel like I'm *running* along this path to independence. And I'm just an average guy—I'm not taking excessive risks on exotic stuff like the futures market, and I still go and work at a job every day. The most important things in my life are my wife and my dogs. I'm not obsessed with making money—but I don't want to worry about it, either.

You can increase your net worth by investing, by reducing spending, by borrowing intelligently to acquire appreciating assets, by giving less to Revenue Canada and by reducing your debts. You can do all that or just part of it. But for God's sake, don't do nothing.

Aim to increase your net worth by 15 percent a year. That should be no big deal. Accountants at Touche Ross calculate that if you're worth $100,000 now, and you achieve 15 percent annual growth, your worth will double every five years. That means you're worth $200,000 in five and $400,000 in ten. Or if you're worth $500,000 now, you could have $2 million by 1998. It's worth shooting for. By the way, Touche Ross has a pretty decent book with some useful ideas in it. I don't agree with some of the investment suggestions, but if you want to know more about net worth and how to expand it, then look for a copy of *Canadian Guide to Personal Financial Management*, (Prentice-Hall, $14.95.)

There are a couple of other investment areas to think about. Mutual funds have been sold aggressively in this country, and an astonishing amount of money has been invested. The average mutual fund holder has put in about $10,000, and many people have used leverage to swing their investment. They borrow the money from the bank, invest, and then, because this is a legitimate investment loan, they're able to write the loan interest off their taxable income.

Too many people, however, borrow to invest merely so they can create this tax advantage. They don't concentrate on the investment aspect, or on how well their fund will perform. In the wake of Black Monday, fortunately, that's starting to change.

Mutual funds are pools of capital put in by hundreds (or thousands) of small investors. The advantage to you is that professional managers invest that money for you, in a whole range of things, with the object of making it grow as much as possible. Supposedly these guys are smarter, or at least more informed, than you are, and the fund will outperform anything you might have done with your own money. Usually that works.

But the mutual funds that were more attractive a year ago and were sold the hardest were "growth" funds, which are heavily invested in stocks. Unfortunately, most of those supposedly smart managers did not see the logic of taking profits before the October crash. As a result, most equity funds (stocks are also called equities) were nailed for about 20 percent of their value—and the experience was even worse in the States. That hit hard at investors who had been on board only for eight or nine months. It wiped out their gains, and when the fees and commissions were taken into account, many of them experienced a sizable loss.

Because of that, investors have been looking for safer harbors, like fixed-income or money market funds. Now the name of the game is not so much to get growth but to preserve wealth, to keep ahead of inflation and enjoy a modest, secure return.

Only in February 1988 did people get a close look at what Black Monday had done to once-trendy mutuals. The Investment Funds Institute of Canada released figures showing that sales of funds had plunged by two-thirds in the last few months of 1987; investors had opted for safe, secure non-stock investments. Net sales in the fourth quarter of the year dived from $1.2 billion in the same period of 1986 to just $421 million. And of that, fully $309 million went into money market funds, which appeal to people who want low risk, a decent but not outrageous return, and the ability to cash out fast.

Money market funds are new to Canada. They invest in Treasury bills, bank notes and high-quality corporate debt. They are an excellent place to hide for people fleeing the stock market. Some of the funds pay daily compound interest and let you take your money out on a single day's notice. In early 1988, these kinds of funds were paying investors between 8 and 9 percent. Considering the current inflation rate, and the liquidity, this is not too shabby.

If you want to invest in mutuals, you're best to stay away from equity ones at least until the stock market establishes some kind of a normal trading pattern (whatever that is). Instead, look at bond and income funds based on real estate or mortgages or even precious metals. All of those survived the stock crash with flying colors. Or you can invest in a mutual fund that spreads the risk around by itself investing in a host of other funds. An example would be the Dynamic Managed Portfolio, which puts money in Canadian equity funds, gold, cash, bonds and foreign funds.

Of great concern is the money it costs you to invest this way. Commissions generally run in the 9 percent range, which is a lot. There can be regular management fees, and there may also be what's indelicately called rear-end loads, which mean paying a substantial amount when you redeem (sell) your units in the fund.

If you are considering a mutual fund, make sure all the costs are spelled out. Take a prospectus home and read it cover to cover. Ask to see literature on comparable funds, and compare them for performance and security—hundreds of these investments are available. Don't be wooed by talk about creating a tax shelter. This is an investment, so there's no point getting a tax break and suffering a loss of your capital at the same time.

Okay, so much for funds. Just watch yourself, and your rear end.

Another hot market is Canadian art. Prices for paintings are rumbling higher. In fact, the Canadian art market has only really developed in earnest within the past seven or eight years, and many believe that prices are still just a fraction of where they should be.

In March of 1987 a Japanese insurance company paid $53.2 million for Vincent van Gogh's *Sunflowers*. The world was shocked and appalled. Then, just eight months later, an anonymous European investor plunked down $71.9 million for another van Gogh—*Irises*—which a lot of people thought wasn't as good as *Sunflowers*. Meanwhile other paintings were starting to get bid up astronomically. A medi-

148

148
Lawren Stewart Harris, O.S.A.
(1885-1970)

MOUNTAIN SKETCH LXV
oil on board
signed and titled by the artist on the reverse
12 by 15 in. *30.5 by 38.1 cm.*
This is a sketch for the large canvas, *Mountains in Snow: Rocky Mountain Paintings, No. VII*, that sold for $450,000.00 at Sotheby's (Canada) on November 18th, 1986, lot 477, establishing a world record for this artist, and also the highest price for a Canadian work sold at auction.

Provenance:
Private Collection, Ottawa

Exhibited:
Lawren S. Harris: Urban Scenes and Wilderness Landscapes 1906-1930, Art Gallery of Ontario, Toronto, January 14th to February 28th, 1978, no. 157.

$40,000-50,000

181

181
Cornelius David Krieghoff
(1815-1872)

INDIAN BASKET SELLER
oil on canvas
signed
(oval) 10½ by 9 in. *26.7 by 22.9 cm.*
The composition of this painting is virtually identical to a work in the collection of The Public Archives of Canada, Ottawa.

Provenance:
Private Collection, Montreal

$35,000-40,000

Two pages from Southeby's auction catalogue of Important Canadian Art. The value of Canadian art has soared over the past five years. One of the superstars is Group of Seven pioneer Lawren Harris, who died in 1970 at the age of 85. This 12" by 15" Harris sketch is valued at $40,000. The larger painting made from the sketch sold in 1986 for a record $450,000. Another hot property is any painting by Cornelius Krieghoff (1815-1972), who chronicled rural Quebec and Indian life. This painting is 10" by 9" and sold at auction in November, 1987 for over $35,000. The value had effectively doubled in five years—and this is a modest price for a Krieghoff.

ocre landscape by John Constable sold for $5 million, for example.

Okay, who can afford that? But the most a Canadian painting ever sold for was $495,000, and that happened in late 1987 when Lawren Harris's huge and majestic *Mountains in Snow: Rocky Mountain Paintings No. VII* changed hands at an auction in Toronto. Of course, you don't need that kind of money to play the game—less than $10,000 can get you into the big leagues.

The best place in the country to buy art, other than private galleries, is at auctions and the biggest seller is Sotheby's, which traditionally holds its sales at the Four Seasons Hotel on Avenue Road in Toronto. If you want to be put on the mailing list and buy catalogues for the sales (themselves appreciating assets), then write: 9 Hazelton Avenue, Toronto M5R 2E1; or call (416) 926-1774.

Here's are some examples of the kind of

price appreciation that's going on. William Kurelek was a western Canadian painter who turned out what were long considered "primitive" depictions of rural life, often laced with weird religious images. The Bank of Nova Scotia has been a big collector. In 1980 the Sotheby's catalogue listed Kurelek paintings for between $2,000 and $6,000. In May of 1987 the listings went from $3,000 to $18,000. By November the cheapest was $8,000, and prices went all the way to $25,000.

Ken Danby is one of the country's foremost realist painters, in the same school as east coast master Alex Colville or naturalist Robert Bateman. In 1980 you could buy a Danby for between $5,000 and $7,000. Now they routinely sell for over $20,000.

The Group of Seven are hot stuff, especially Lawren Harris, who had a fixation with the landscape of northern Ontario and the Rockies. His style was unique and his paintings are breathtaking. So are the prices. In 1980 a Harris was selling for between $18,000 and $24,000. Now a small sketch costs at least $12,000, and the large paintings sell for $30,000 to $100,000. With that blockbuster sale in November 1987, new price levels have been established.

The value of Canadian art is rapidly escalating, and there is every reason to believe more increases are in store. People with bank accounts and bare walls should think hard about it. As with everything else, however, don't run off half-cocked. Learn about the subject. Take a course or buy some informative books. Browse in public galleries before you haunt the commercial ones. Beware of the $49.95 "starving artist" sales held at Ramada Inns on Sundays. And make sure any art you're buying can be authenticated. You would not believe the number of Americans, for example, who paid big bucks for Salvador Dali "prints" that turned out to be posters.

Finally, why spend money on depreciating furniture when you can spend it on appreciating antiques? The price of good Canadian antique furniture has soared over the past five years, and there is now a genuine shortage of certain pieces, particularly early Quebec pine and quality Ontario pre-Confederation crocks. Dorothy's store sells a lot of pine. A year ago she could buy a flat-to-the-wall pine cupboard for $700. Now she's lucky to find one for under $3,000. It will not be long before the auction price is close to $5,000. American dealers come up and buy whatever they see, at almost any price. Compared with the value of U.S. antique furniture, ours is vastly underpriced.

If you need chairs to sit on, don't buy them new and watch them turn into used furniture. Instead, invest. Find a nice set of ladderbacks or Windsors or hoopbacks. Don't buy a new dresser for your bedroom; get a bonnet chest instead. Use a dovetailed pine blanket box for linen storage. Put a jam cupboard in your kitchen to store dishes and use a dry sink to put your telephone on. And how about a nice armoire for the television, stereo and VCR? (I'm not trying to pump up Dorothy's business, honest.)

So clearly, even with something as mundane as your home furnishings, it's possible to earn money rather than just spend it.

Chapter Six

Who's zoomin' who? Mike Wilson's tax reform

Across from Lansdowne Stadium in Ottawa sits one of the lousiest restaurants on the planet. It's more a watering hole than anything else. The beer is supplemented by greasy sandwiches and acrid fries. The waitresses look like hookers.

Just after noon on June 18, 1987, I was sitting in this miserable place, looking out the dirty window at the stadium. A few tables away were three gigantic guys, players for the Ottawa Roughriders having a bite before practice. The waitresses knew them by name.

Attached to the stadium is the Ottawa Convention Centre, the scene of steamy political leadership conventions and the usual fare of trade shows. I knew that once I went in, past the security guards, I'd be in there until eight that night. So I sat in this horrible restaurant and listened to the ball players say lewd things to women who were enjoying it.

Inherently, I hate lock-ups. It's routine in Ottawa, where the feds try to aggrandize everything by incarcerating journalists for hours with simplistic documents. It happens every February with the budget, which is more understandable because there can be hundreds of changes contained in one of those. That day I didn't know what to expect.

For most of the past two years Finance Minister Mike Wilson had been talking about tax reform. Suddenly the Americans had done it, ushering in what Ronald Reagan called "the second American revolution." For months and months the Yanks debated and honed the proposals; lobby groups commented and newspaper editorials criticized. Then, in a surprise compromise, Congress and the Senate hammered out a reform package, and sweeping changes went into effect with the 1987 taxation year. It was the typical U.S. approach—open, upfront and democratic.

Mike Wilson would do the typical Canadian thing. This day, would stand up in the House of Commons, deliver a nationally televised speech and dump an incomprehensible array of changes on the heads of the Canadian people. The next day acres of newspaper copy would try to explain in human language what the hell it all meant. The debate, if any, would come afterwards. Instead of inviting public input at the decision-making stage, the feds would challenge the country to prove why everything they'd done wasn't perfect. This system has never served Canada well, and it still doesn't.

Around one o'clock I couldn't take the dive any longer, and crossed the street to the stadium. I checked in with the guards and signed a document saying I wouldn't try to escape before they let me out. I collected my package of information on tax reform and wandered into the main room where hundreds of reporters, artists, T.V. technicians and hangers-on milled about. Computers, tax reform booklets, paper cups and food littered the long tables. The finance department had arranged a buffet in there, knowing that most journalists can be bought off with a fresh muffin.

I found the *Toronto Sun* camp and asked assistant managing editor John Paton, one of the saner people in this business, how the package looked.

"This is a crock of shit," he said. I decided to go and get some free food.

Tax reform had become a global reality, coming down in country after country and reflecting a new economic reality. Economics are now driven by consumers, through service-sector industries. Smokestacks are giving way to computer screens. Assembly lines are run by microcomputers, not hands. When governments cannot tax robotics, they have to adjust the tax base. They reform. Once the Americans pulled their tax reform act together, Ottawa had to follow suit. U.S. corporate taxes would now be lower, and multinationals had a powerful incentive to move operations south of the border.

Eighteen months after saying the tax system needed some work, Wilson unveiled a dramatic package of changes. The man had been saying for months that tax reform would simplify the system. It would be fairer. And it would be "revenue neutral"—that is, it would not increase taxation. All of those claims turned out to be lies.

The package painted a dark picture of rising taxes, dwindling opportunities to escape them, the dawn of taxes on capital gains, punitive treatment for the middle class, special punishment for the self-employed and the spectre of a wildly inflationary national sales tax touching everything from food and housing to haircuts and cars.

In return for this, Wilson was simplifying tax brackets and enacting a small (average $400 a year) personal tax cut. The bad news was that this in no way compensated for the 100 percent increase in taxes since the Mulroney Tories had come to power. And despite that, Wilson was still projecting a $30 billion deficit for the fiscal year. Since 1984, even with all those tax hikes, our federal debt had risen by about $100 billion. A shameful record. Obviously the government had shown no resolve at all in cutting spending. After three successive rounds of stiff tax hikes we were, as a nation, worse off than ever. And now we had a tax "reform" in which taxes would be sharply increased, with no promise that the government would try to put its house in order.

In Japan tax reform came down on October 28, 1986, after a year-long effort to change a system that had been in effect since 1950. The reform proposed by Prime Minister Yasuhiro Nakasone turned out to be a virtual model for Wilson's plan eight months later. It lowered personal tax rates, hit corporations a bit harder, rid the system of inducements to save and introduced a comprehensive, national, indirect, multistage sales tax.

Suddenly, all hell broke loose. Led by opposition parties and organized labor, the streets of Japanese cities overflowed with protestors. One march attracted 500,000 people; Nakasone was carried in effigy and publicly humiliated. A whole society could not believe that virtually all they would consume would be subject to tax. The government slipped in the polls, from a 53 percent approval rate in late 1986 to a disastrous 24 percent by March 1987. Nakasone started to backtrack, saying the sales tax proposal could be modified. In April his party suffered heavily in nationwide, midterm elections. Within days,

Nakasone ditched the tax reform package.

The contrast with Canada could not be more telling. There were no Canadian howls of protest, other than some limp-wristed criticism of the government's plans to tax food. Those plans have since been scrapped—food and drugs will be exempt.) Lobby groups try to show that a consumption tax will add $16,000 to the price of a $200,000 home, but the message falls on deaf Canadian ears.

When I walked into the tax reform lock-up, I expected several things. Among them were lower personal tax brackets, and fewer of them, the ditching of most exemptions and deductions, the beginning of the end for the capital gains tax holiday and a national sales tax.

In fact, tax reform without a national sales tax would not have been reform. It would only have been a budget-like tinkering with existing rules. Wilson would have to put a revenue-generator like that in place, I thought, before he could substantially change the rest of the game. It would shift the burden of tax from earners to consumers, as potentially dangerous as that could be in a country fuelled by department store, house and car sales.

The first thing John Paton told me was that Wilson hadn't done that. Instead, the feds were going to usher in tax reform in two pieces, a grab-bag of changes to the old rules first and a consumption tax later—much later, perhaps into the 1990s. As I sat down to study the material, I already doubted this was going to be any different from a regular budget. But it was. It was worse. And that's why I did something a lot of my colleagues had a hard time with: I got involved.

Once a generation you get a chance to do something like rewrite all the tax rules. It hadn't happened for seventeen years, and this was Wilson's opportunity. The tax system was a mess, and it was unfair. It also wasn't raising enough cash to satisfy the government's appetite for spending. Already we had surtaxes at the federal and provincial levels, a new minimum tax, outrageously inflated sin taxes on booze and tobacco, and three solid years of budgetary tax increases. It would have been politically unpalatable for Wilson to hike them again. So he took his once in a political lifetime opportunity for genuine reform, and he turned it into a dirty little weapon against the Canadian middle class.

The tax reform material upset me at first and continued to disturb me over the following days. I wrote several newspaper columns about reform in the early summer of 1987. It bothered me that such important stuff was being brought in just as Canada went on summer vacation. And the media had been lazy. They gave big headlines to Wilson's statements before June 18 saying tax reform would leave more money in most people's paycheques. There was a one-day flurry of coverage after the event, and then zippo. As a consequence, most Canadians didn't have the foggiest clue what tax reform really meant. They vaguely approved because they had only vague knowledge. Few realized the implications for the middle class.

The feds were doing all they could to slide the package by. The June launch, just when Canadians were packing off for summer holidays, was followed by an August 18 deadline for public submissions—about the most unlikely time of the year for a mass response. After that the House of Commons finance committee would hold some public hearings and submit a report in mid-November. The whole mess was to come into effect with the 1988 tax year, which meant there would be no time left for any meaningful debate. But this kind of reform *demanded* extensive public debate. And then the opposition parties completely dropped the ball, and tax reform—misunderstood by them, as well—sailed through the Commons.

I did not want this whole process to happen without at least some ankle-biting. So I told my readers that if they wanted, I'd represent their interests before the finance committee. I wrote a column on tax reform and at the bottom inserted two coupons. One had the headline "Mr. Wilson, It's Good Stuff;" the other was headed "Mr. Wilson, I Don't Like It." Each included a few lines for comments and asked for a name and an address.

Those were published in one newspaper, by one columnist. Frankly, I thought a response of five hundred on the topic of tax reform, during an intense summer heat wave, when most people were on holiday, and just following a national postal strike would have been satisfactory. It would have given me a fair sampling of opinion. Instead, the replies numbered seven thousand. They came from central Quebec, across southern Ontario, from Winnipeg, Calgary and Edmonton. Over three thousand came with letters, some of them long and thoughtful. I was sent petitions collected at corner stores and on the floor of the General Motors plant in Oshawa. I was sent coupons that had been put through the office copier so everyone at work could fill one out.

Mike Wilson had said he was going to change all the rules. But it took weeks for the reality of tax reform to hit home to the average Canadian. Few of us realized at first just how massive the proposed changes were. Fewer still saw the inherent unfairness of Wilson's move to a "fairer, more equitable" system.

Canadians will stomach more tax, but not when it comes without benefit. Not when the mortgage on the future keeps increasing mindlessly. Tax reform was clearly a crime against the country. "Every dollar of your savings will be subject to tax," I wrote in a newspaper column a few weeks prior to the cut-off day. "Kids over 18 won't get you a tax break. The capital gains tax holiday will be ending. Most car expenses will be disallowed. The middle class will pay 50 percent more tax than those low wage-earners, while the wealthy will pay only 9 percent more then the middle.

"Over the past few days I have asked readers to raise their voices on the issue of reform. So far several thousand of them have written me, and more letters are pouring in daily. All of this will form part of our submission to the federal government and, with any luck, the feds will allow your reporter to deliver it in person."

The vast majority of responses were articulate, angry and fully aware of what Ottawa was trying to pull off under the cover of a sleepy summer. This is a sampling of what Canadians had to say:

I am self-employed and work six days a week trying to scratch out a living. I voted for Mulroney in the last election because you were supposed to be the champions of small business.

Your new proposals will effectively double my tax payable and put my net income below the poverty line! I have contributed through my previous company and personally to the federal and provincial PC parties within my means. However, if these tax changes go through,

I will not vote PC under any circumstances in the next election.

Jack Pitt, Oakville

I am angered that as one of the middle class, holding a full-time job, which I augment through an entrepreneurial bent, I am now threatened with being penalized for my ambition.

It is my hope that if enough of us respond to your call to action we can make a change in pending legislation. I call for everyone who is as angered as I am to promise to vote these people out of office if they continue to attack the strength of this country, the middle class.

Elizabeth Shropshire, Mississauga

It seems government is no longer content to nickle-and dime us to death. It's now going for the jugular. Tax planning seems to be a thing of the past. Incentives for saving and investing are almost non-existent, for the new strategy seems to be "take it all!"

I don't mind a little short-term pain for long-term gain. I think anyone who has had any success today has experienced this. But the new regime would have us suffer the pain to the end of our days. The original question you asked was simple. So is the answer: Mr. Wilson, I don't like it!

William Brunow, Toronto

Where on earth is a political party which is truly conservative? One that believes in personal freedom and the free enterprise system? In the not-too-distant future, if we don't smarten up, we will all be working for the government for a full year, not just the half-year it takes now to pay for all the various taxes. We will become (as we are fast becoming) a Third World nation.

Mediocrity will replace excellence. Who will run a business, take a risk—if everything you work for is taken away in taxes to support your neighbor who chooses not to work? I was once proud to be a Canadian—but no more. Hard work and initiative are penalized in this country and the lazy and the cheaters are rewarded.

Joan Busbridge, Scarborough

Who is Wilson trying to nail? The businessman like me who works seven days a week in order to be financially free in my old age? I'm losing my incentive, my motivation. Doesn't he realize that if I become successful I'll have to hire more people just to keep up with the demand? And they'll pay income tax!

Steve Macko, Oshawa

As an accountant, all I can say is, as a reform of our tax system, it stinks, and almost 100 percent of my clientele is prepared to say, "forget it, who need this? I'll quit working 18 hours a day and get a job in the post office." I guess then, at least, they'd have the right to strike against the government.

L.R.Vernon, Richmond Hill

Do you really think the average, working middle-class person is going to like you, Mr. Wilson, taking their interest on their savings account? The interest on savings is our reward for having survived all your other taxes, and struggling to get ahead in this government-eaten world.

C. Mason, Stouffville

On and on and on the letters went. They showed a strong grasp of the complex issues at hand. They showed the Canadian middle class clinging to its dream of personal financial independence. And they told me of a deep adversarial feeling toward government and politicians.

Through this, the only public sampling in the country on the issue of tax reform, a single word was repeated endlessly, from thousands of lips: "betrayal."

Of the responses I received, 99.6 percent of them were against the tax reform package. All these people were united in defending the right of someone in this country to make it on their own. Tax reform proposals to increase capital gains and make life harder for the self-employed clearly ran counter to the spirit of the people. Worse, they ran against the philosophy of the Tory party itself. It had only been two years earlier when Mike Wilson, on a budget night, said he wanted to rustle the entrepreneurial spirit. That day he gave the little guy something to shoot for—he unveiled a $500,000 lifetime capital gains tax exemption.

Now tax reform capped that exemption at just $100,000. It also moved to increase the way capital gains were taxed. Starting in 1989, two-thirds of any individual gain would be taxed. After that, three-quarters.

Increasingly, capital gains will be taxed like regular income—at the high personal rate. Not only is this wrong but it runs directly counter to a "conservative" view of the economy. There are significantly greater risks involved in earning a capital gain than in, say, just collecting your paycheque. Not offering a corresponding greater reward is nuts. It kills any incentive investors might feel to put their money at risk, whether it's buying stock in a Canadian company or starting up a variety store. And without investment, we're cooked. We might as well let the Americans or Japanese come in and do it for us.

Tax reform made me angry. It still does.

On a sunny morning in late September I set out for the airport, only to find that the 401 had turned into a massive parking lot. A tractor-trailer had jackknifed, and I had to drive down the highway shoulder, across a median, up an exit ramp and across a concession road to reach the airport in the nick of time—to find my plane had been delayed. By the time we were airborne, I was perilously late. If I missed my 11 a.m. appearance before the committee, there would be no re-run. A big newspaper audience would have been let down. The trouble with setting yourself up as a public figure is that you have to deliver the goods.

I gave the cabbie an extra twenty-dollar bill to drive like a bandit to the West Block. As I walked into the committee room I breathed a sign of relief, seeing the group before me was running five minutes late. A Canadian Press photographer took some pictures of me sitting in the witness chair, beside committee chairman Don Blenkarn, who guffawed and chortled and made his face look happy. As soon as the CP guy left, Blenkarn wiped the congeniality away, took his station at the other end of the room and, before I'd said anything, told me to be brief. He looked at his watch, settled back and looked away.

Back in my Toronto office early that evening I churned out this report:

Room 209 of the West Block of the Parliament buildings has a thick wooden door taking you into an ugly room dominated by a big oval table, a Canadian flag, and Don Blenkarn.

This is where the House of Commons finance committee hangs out. Over the past few weeks an endless stream of professional business, labor and economic groups have been pulling the door open and seeing the table, the flag, the man. This morning he has tousled gray hair, white shirt sleeves and two empty plastic coffee cups sitting in front.

Around the table are people like Liberal Aideen Nicholson, Tory Geoff Wilson and NDPer Simon De Jong. In this room there are very few observers, and almost no media reporters. Yet here the crucial issue of tax reform is being debated. This is the only chance Canadians get to try to change the rules, before they change life as we know it.

Around the table are jet-black microphones with little red lights on them. When someone speak, the light flashes on and from behind a white plastic wall a woman's voice can be heard translating the words.

As I entered Room 209 yesterday morning the Quebec Chamber of Commerce was making its case, asking that the government not go ahead with tax reform in two parts—personal and corporate changes first, a new sales tax second. The chamber was also coming in for some heavy sailing.

After intense questioning—which he was winning—De Jong leaned forward and asked, "What visions of Canada do you have?" The chamber spokesman hesitated.

Blenkarn laughed.

The witness, flanked by three supporters, was now chain-smoking. It was not going well.

A moment later Blenkarn called a recess. I was on in three minutes.

What followed yesterday was an extrtaordinary 1 1/4 hour session. You and I—after submission of our brief containing the names and comments of thousands of people—were given almost twice as long to testify as any other delegation to these hearings.

It was not a love-in

Blenkarn started it off by giving me five minutes to make my case. At the end of that time, and while I was attempting to read some of your letters into the record, he cut me off. Then he started to ask a question which sounded a hell of a lot like a speech. I did not answer it. Instead I said if the committee was not interested in listening then I would save my breath, come back and let you know.

Blenkarn retreated, only to attack again.

This time he pulled out a column I'd written weeks earlier on another issue—the fact Revenue Canada is now enforcing rules to apply capital gains on principal residences that rest on large acreages.

"Haven't you deliberately tried to show the government's gone out of its way to beat on the little people?" he asked.

This was a cheap diversionary tactic, of course, and I tried to skate around it. The man is not an easy foe.

Well, friends, the heat continued for several minutes. There was clearly more interest at first in discrediting the messenger than listening to the message. But soon the tide turned.

Soon a majority of committee members present were coming to understand that the middle class—the people whose names stuffed my five-binder presentation—worried about more than the price of beer. They care about government spending, about the deficit, about the costs of debt, and the fact taxes keep going up because politicians can neither manage the economy nor make tough decisions.

"Thank you," Geoff Wilson said, "for bringing this to us. And I am glad to hear you saying those things. My concerns are exactly that, but I thought people didn't give a damn about the debt or the deficit."

By now the binders filled with your coupons and letters were scrambled around the big oval table. Members of the committee were reading and turning pages and they were absorbed with what they saw there—as I had been a month earlier. Don Blenkarn was admitting that we "obviously' have a problem in Canada.

"Either we're not collecting enough taxes, or we're spending too much. What would you do?"

I told him that readers thought the government-slashing measures of the Nielson task force had been ignored. That the Forget commissions on ways to reduce UIC rip-offs had been shelved. That many people questioned the defence budget and especially our foreign aid program. And forgiving $325 million in loans to several French-speaking African counries sent out all the wrong signals.

Blenkarn said those were unrepayable loans anyway, which the government had written off a year ago. Wilson said even making cuts in all those areas amounted to "peanuts." And I said we are but taxpayers and citizens. We don't hold the budgetary strings. We are not privy to the many bottom lines which make up government.

But what we do know is that for the first century of its life, Canada held together, paid the bills and survived. And now, in the space of just a handful of years, we have a $260 billion debt and a $30-billion-a-year budget shortfall.

And we know that's not good enough.

Blenkarn was nodding in agreement. And, well, we went on. About how a car should be a business tool for a salesperson, not a perk. About how increasing capital gains taxes just robbed people of incentive. And about the new consumption tax, De Jong agreed: It will be inflationary and it will reduce consumption.

"It hits the middle class, the average small-business person. It's the ability of these people to consume which creates the economic engine of growth. You need the dollars flowing from down below."

I also told the Tories on this committee that you feel they, in particular, have betrayed you. They promised responsibility, and have not delivered. We have higher taxes *and* higher debt.

Seventy minutes after Blenkarn cut me short and then tried to cut me up, he came over to speak personally. So did several other committee members, and either they are slick politicians or they honestly cared about your submission. Yesterday we got no promises or assurances of change. But we got a hearing. We showed the middle class cares more about this country than it gets credit for. We want neither a mortgage on our future nor empty phrases today.

I was proud of yesterday. We are easy to ignore. We're just the people, not the leaders.

But it didn't happen.

For weeks afterwards I got notes and phone calls from people who appreciated having their name put on that table. I can't tell you how many times I'd answer the phone and somebody would say, "I'm just a reader. Thank you for representing me."

It's hard to overstate the disdain that ordinary working Canadians feel for politicians. Most people want to be left alone. They don't want welfare, unemployment benefits or government-assisted housing. Most Canadians are surprisingly independent and self-reliant. Yet most politicians don't have a clue about this. They listen only to the lobby groups and the special interest groups, and so the majority of us have to live with government policies that are all aimed at the fringes. One group lobbies for a national daycare program to help single working mothers and suddenly the whole country is looking at annual costs running into the billions. And the majority of middle-class Canadians sincerely don't believe that looking after kids is the state's responsibility.

Anyway, the middle class does not have lobbyists in Ottawa the way the Canadian Manufacturers' Association, the Canadian Federation of Labor or the National Action Committee on the Status of Women do. No, we make the mistake of thinking the people we elect will lobby on our behalf against wrong-minded laws or changes that wound us morally or financially.

It ain't so. Most of them don't have the guts to stand up against the special interests, the party line or members of Cabinet. As a result, this country is skating on ice so thin you can reach through it. Nothing—not a person, a corporation or a government—can exist for long when it keeps borrowing more money each year. Tax reform was an example of an ongoing economic mistake. Rather than address government spending, the feds came up with a way to screw more money out of the middle class and to establish the framework for a national tax that steals over $15 billion a year from the economy.

And while doing that, they plan on greatly accelerating our debt position. Tax reform documents admit that our debt will be over $400 billion by 1991. Four years ago it was under $200 billion. What will it be when your new baby is starting school—close to a trillion dollars? And how much of his income will he have to give over in adulthood to keep the country alive? Seventy percent? More?

The second century for this country is not shaping up too well. We are on the same course that Argentina was on a decade ago. Now its middle class is decimated, its currency ruined, its economy shattered. That country faces a very uncertain political future. Could this be Canada in the late 1990s? When we're borrowing money each year to pay the interest on last year's debt, what else can the future hold for the middle classe who want less government, not more?

I can't answer these questions. I wish I knew someone in government who could. Political leadership has gone down the tubes here. We have managers, not visionaries. We have people who make politics a self-serving career, instead of looking at public life as public service.

The tax reform experience made me bitter. We got a new set of rules without consultation. There was hardly any public debate. The changes were never well enough explained. And it should have been Mike Wilson touring the country hearing what real, warm taxpayers think—not Blenkarn.

Many of the tax reforms are destructive. They are mean-spirited and petty. They take special aim at self-employed Canadians, when we should be doing all we can to encourage risk-taking as a way to salvage our sinking economy. Sadly, tax reform is going to hasten the economic decline of Canada.

And reform makes it more important than ever that you should build a shelter against the future.

Tax reform involves a ton of changes. This book could talk about nothing else, but that would be pretty boring. There's more to life than taxes, after all.

At the end of this chapter I've listed some names, addresses and phone numbers you can use to get more information on tax reform. Some of these books and booklets even come at the right price—free. Tax reform was to Canada's accounting profession just about what World War Two was to the military. This was the big one. This was what all the training had been for. As a result, the country's major firms have spent thousands of hours interpreting, analyzing, dissecting and regurgitating tax reform. Almost all of them have published material on the changes, some of it exhaustive. Some of it is even understandable. My list includes only the stuff I think can help you.

Without much further editorial comment, let's run through some of the major changes.

•In 1987 we had ten tax brackets. Now we have three. If you earn less than $27,500 a year, your rate is 17 percent. On the next $27,500, the rate jumps to 26 percent. And on that portion of your income above $55,000, the rate is 29 percent. You may well ask why people earning wages in the middle range would have to pay a much higher rate than the under-$27,500 crowd and yet very close to the over-$55,000 group. It would be a good question, too, because it shows exactly how the middle class is being nailed on Mike Wilson's cross.

However, the feds insist that with the new, slightly-lower tax brackets, most people will take home more money, probably starting around the middle of 1988. They also say that about 850,000 taxpayers will be dropped entirely from the tax rolls. But before you get too excited about that, it's worth noting that tax changes brought in since 1984 were largely responsible for putting them on the rolls in the first place.

The three tax rates are, in fact, a little higher, since we still have a 3 percent surtax in effect. That brings the top rate to just about 30 percent, compared with a top rate of 35 percent before tax reform. However, taxable income after tax reform could actually be much higher because ...

•All personal exemptions and deductions have been changed into tax credits. So you might find yourself heading quickly into a higher tax bracket. As bean-counters at Deloitte, Haskins & Sells point out, somebody earning $35,000 would, with the old system of deductions and exemptions fall into the 17 percent bracket. But when credits replace those, the tax rate jumps to 26 percent. There is obviously more here than meets the eye.

And let's not forget that provincial taxes are added on to federal ones and raise the effective rate of taxation. Ontario, for example, charges you 50 percent of whatever the feds do.

In general, people with lower incomes will find that the system of tax credits is good to them. But people in middle- and upper-income ranges will be hurt for the value of the credits will be significantly lower than the value of the personal exemptions. But with the slightly lower tax brackets, there's a good chance things might equal out.

The $500 employment expense deduction is now history. But some things stay—like deductions for moving expenses, child care expenses and alimony payments. And there continue to be tax credits for RRSP contributions, donations to political parties and for having children.

•One of the worst things that can happen to you is to have your income push you from the 17 percent bracket up into the 26 percent one. This works out to represent about 14 percent more in tax—and where are you going to get a 14 percent jump in income these days? If your income is floating close to $30,000—make sure you maximize all the ways to reduce your taxable income. Dump all you can into RRSPs each year and claim that credit. You might also want to borrow to make investments, because the interest on your investment loans is deductible from taxable income.

•Gone is the $1,000 interest and dividend income deduction, which means that all the interest your savings earn is now taxable. Given the relatively low rates that have been available lately, this means you have to look aggressively for new places to stash your wealth.

•Tax reform does a lot to the way capital gains are, and will be, taxed. You'll remember how the treatment of capital gains was a centrepiece of Tory economic policy just a few years ago. Now the attitude has changed substantially, and the move is on to start treating these gains just as if they were regular income.

A capital gain is the profit you get when you cash out of an investment. Unlike regular paycheque income, this money comes as a result of a one-time deal—like buying a stock at $10 a share and selling it at $20. Or profiting from appreciations in the price of gold, art or (in some cases) real estate. (Revenue Canada has been trying to treat proceeds from "speculative" real estate deals as income, not capital gains, and the courts seem to be supporting that view.)

Right now you get to keep half the profit you make, and you pay tax on the other half, according to your personal tax rate. Starting next year you'll be paying tax on two-thirds of the gain, and by 1990, on three-quarters of the gain. As I've said elsewhere, this is a foolish move. Earning a capital gain almost always involves taking a risk. If the return is diminished by taxes, then so is the incentive to try.

By the way, capital gains made from the sale of your principal residence remain free of tax. You can designate one principal residence in a taxation year; and a spouse can no longer claim another one—as long as you're living together, that is.

•The federal government has also started to moon walk on the $500,000 lifetime capital gains exemption it unveiled with much fanfare not that long ago. The limit has now been capped at $100,000, and the whole thing may not survive much longer at all. The hundred grand is the whole amount of your gain, not just the taxable part. And it's cumulative, which means if you used $40,000 last year, you only have $60,000 left. (This has nothing to do with your principal residence.)

There are two important exceptions. If you own qualified farm property, you can sell it and claim up to $500,000 as a capital gains exemption. And, since January 1, 1988, the sale of shares in a small business corporation can also net you the full exemption. How long this will last, however, is anybody's guess. On the other side of the coin, you can suffer capital losses and carry them forward into other years to offset gains then. But the investment loss rules can be complicated, depending on your situation. Refer to the material at the end of this chapter for the gory technical details.

•It's important to remember that money flowing into your hands is taxed in different ways. Your paycheque is taxed as regular income, and one of the three federal tax brackets applies, depending on how much you earn. Interest income is now fully taxed the same way. Dividends are taxed more lightly. In fact in 1986 you could have received $40,000 a year in dividend income and paid no tax. Now that's down into the $22,000 range. Capital gains we've touched upon; they are also less taxed than regular income and interest income.

Finally, there is cash, which can change hands and escape taxation—something that's happening more frequently. I know a guy who is a millionaire and deals almost exclusively in cash. Revenue Canada suspects him, but so far has been unable to prove anything. He faced an audit several years ago and managed to confound tax officials by not having a single piece of paper—on anything. He was ordered to keep a record of his cash transactions, and so rummaged up from the trash the worst-looking soiled scribbler he could find. Every month he'd make a few chicken scratches in it, put on his worst clothes and take it to the tax office. Soon they asked him to stop coming.

• It can make sense to borrow money for investment purposes, rather than use your own. Interest on money invested in something that produces income is deductible from taxable income. But this doesn't mean you can borrow $150,000 to buy a piece of rental real estate yielding $600 a month in rent, just to claim an $18,000 annual interest expense. Revenue Canada says there has to be a reasonable expectation of profit. If you try to set up a situation to give you tax-deductible losses, forget it. The courts have already shot that one down. But if you borrow fully to invest in something like stocks, you get to write off the interest incurred each year you own them, and that helps save on taxes. When you sell the stock, you can claim the capital gain as part of your lifetime exemption.

• If you bought this book to find out about all kinds of tax shelters, well, I'm sorry. One-by-one they have been falling by the wayside as the government wages war on ways to avoid taxation. murbs (Multiple Unit Residential Buildings), home ownership savings plans, hobby farms, research and development credits, movie investments—they are all gone, going or significantly reduced. The only real way that most Canadians can continue to shelter income is with an RRSP.

Here's the scoop. The Canada Pension Plan is just over twenty years old. In that time it has managed to sink about $30 billion into debt. At the same time, the population is getting older. Fast. Not so long ago just one in ten Canadians was over sixty-five. Within thirty years or so, one in four will be retired. Starting in 1987, CPP deductions on your paycheque began going up, and they will increase every year. But serious doubts linger about the system's abiltiy to hold together and pay pensions to everybody who'll be demanding them. As financial consultant Tom Delaney puts it: "Will future generations of taxpayers be willing to make the so-called intergenerational transfers of wealth? Clearly the long-term future of the public retirement income system is uncertain."

It sure is. When I hit sixty-five in the year 2014, I would be foolish to expect to live on a government pension. What this means, of course, is that individual Canadians have to make sure they have their own resources. Especially at risk now are the Boomies, that bulge in the population that once glutted schools, then competed for summer jobs and in retirement will put huge demands on the system.

The hard way to guarantee comfort when you are an old snort is to get rich soon and stay in that condition. You can do that through successful investing—the two best bets, as we've seen, are small business and real estate. The key is to stabilize your costs and ensure a regular income.

The most important cost to stabilize is that of shelter, and you can do that by owning, rather than renting, real estate. The best kind of income is that which reflects any changes in the cost of living. It's important to realize that we face a potentially huge inflation problem, as governments try to moderate crushing debts by printing more money.

One way around this geriatric hassle is to take advantage of the only meaningful tax dodge left for individual Canadians—the RRSP. I know, this is hardly dynamic and aggressive investing. It's not up there with, say, putting together an ace real estate deal, or the opening day of your new store.

But RRSPS are going to be critically important to this generation, especially now that we are in the era of tax reform. In the environment I've been describing, RRSPS are especially important as tax-saving devices, as well as a path to a dignified retirement. They were first designed to give people who didn't have private pension plans a chance to build up a kind of trust fund for themselves. The money you contribute to a plan each year can be deducted from your taxable income, and that nets you a tax shelter. Better still, the interest or capital gain that your investment earns, once stuck into an RRSP, can stay in there without being taxed. Only when you cash out do the feds stick it to you.

If you're smart, you'll cash in your RRSPS when you are making less money and are, therefore, in a lower tax bracket. This can happen when you're retired. Or it can happen when you are unemployed, when you leave the workforce to have a kid or go back to school or whatever. If can also happen for your wife or hubs. The law allows you not only to contribute to your own plan but also to a spousal one. More on that shortly.

The stats are these: If you work for a company that has a pension plan, then in 1988 you can contribute a max of $3,500. If you are self-employed or work for a company without a plan, then you get to contribute up to $7,500. It's worth noting that about two-thirds of all Canadians fall into this category—and are the people most at risk. The deadline for making a contribution that qualifies for the previous tax year is the end of February. That's why, during that month, the newspapers are drenched with RRSP ads—it's prime time for the investment community.

These contribution maximums are criminally low. Twice already the feds have promised to raise them, and higher limits were supposed to be in place months and months ago. But the latest revision delays the hike until the 1989 taxation year, at which time the $7,500 goes to $8,500, then gradually rises to $15,500 in 1995.

You are allowed to have several plans going at the same time, and you can take some money out by transferring funds into another fund and then cashing out what's left in the old one. But beware: When you collapse an RRSP, the bank or trust company or broker must, by law, keep some of the money back to pay tax. Up to $5,000, and you lose 10 percent, between that and $15,000, it's 20 percent; and above $15,000 the amount withheld rises to 30 percent.

You can put money into your husband or wife's plan, as long as you don't exceed the annual limit for yourself. This makes dandy sense if your spouse earns less than you do and has a lower personal tax rate. But, being crafty, the boys at the finance department have ruled that the spouse has to keep the money in the plan for at least three years, or the contribution is taxed at (egads!) the contributor's rate. This prevents people from running income through a less-taxed husband or wife.

Also gone is the one-time bonanza of being able to borrow money for an RRSP and write the loan interest off your taxable income. Now the cost of borrowing must be borne out of after-tax income, which is a complete drag. However, it can still make some sense to buy an RRSP with invested money if you do it the right way: borrow and invest just before the deadline. That way you will need to carry the loan for a few months less. Then take your tax refund cheque and use it to pay down the loan. Now your RRSP should earn the equivalent of your loan payments—so the investment really costs you nothing.

But how do you know what kind of an RRSP to buy? Look at the papers—there are thousands of them.

Basically decide what kind of risk you want to take. Low-risk plans invest in guaranteed investment certificates or simple bank deposits. Or you can get a mortgage-backed security (Cannie Mae) and put it in a plan. Lately those have been paying very attractive interest.

Higher-risk (especially since Black Monday) are equity-based mutual funds. The selling tactics are often high-pressure, but so is the white knuckle factor. Less risky are mortgage-based mutual funds. Or you can get RRSPS based on bonds, Treasury bills or Canada Savings Bonds. The key to doing all this is to have a self-directed RRSP, which you can easily tailor to your own needs, desires, fears and dreams. You can set up a self-directed plan anywhere the other kinds are sold. You don't need any special legal or accounting help, and annual administration fees run around $100. Just make sure you realize that the risk level could be higher than for a savings plan, depending on what you end up investing in.

Finally, because there are so many plans and their features change each season, let me refer you to financial consultant Tom Delaney. Since the mid-1970s, Delaney has published an annual survey of all these plans available to Canadians. Every year the feds manage to screw things up with a new federal budget, and every year Delaney puts out a new book to stay current. Check the bookstore for *The Delaney Report on RRSPs*. It's worth the $13 it will set you back.

One of the curious things about tax reform is that self-employed people will, by the government's own admission, pay more tax on incomes that match an employee's. (In fact, employees with very high incomes will fare the best, since the top-bracket tax rates fall. Self-employed people could find themselves losing substantially as the effects of tax reform become clear. It's estimated that somebody who earns $75,000 from a combination of commissions, dividend income, capital gains and so on will end up paying about $1,500 more tax than before reform because harsher tax treatment of dividends, stiff new rules for writing off car expenses, reduced entertainment and meal deductions and the virtual elimination of home office expenses. If you are self-employed and earn between $40,000 and $80,000 a year, you can expect to pay at least $1,000 more.

Now, this is hardly fair, because the self-employed person does not have the stability or benefits of a salaried employee. Besides, self-employed people tend to be entrepreneurs who—if they're successful—create jobs for other people. The feds are doing exactly the wrong thing by bringing in these changes, and it will come to haunt them. That no federal politician of note has brought this matter up shows how little the free enterprise spirit burns on Parliament Hill. That's sad.

•Self employed people who deduct home office expenses from the income are in for a shock. Tax reform puts the boots to this, in a move that affects a lot of real estate and insurance agents, doctors, accountants, lawyers—in fact, anyone who works out of their home.

It used to be that all expenses relating to the operation of a home office were fair deductions, whether or not that office was used all the time. But now you're allowed to claim only a portion of those expenses, and—worse—the office has to be your main place of business. That means if you have a desk somewhere else, you're out of luck. This really hits certain professional groups like real estate people, who are on call almost all the time and very often do 90 percent of their work from home. But if the company they work for has a spot for them in the office, all home expenses are disallowed.

Highly unfair, but Finance Minister Mike Wilson said he did it to curb abuses of the old system. One way around this is to incorporate, then charge your company a rent for the use of home office space. The company could, in turn, write off the rent as a legitimate business expense.

•Tax reform complicates the way self-employed people will want to take money out of their companies. In general, if you own and manage a company with an income less than $200,000, then it will probably be to your advantage to take a salary out, making sure to dump the maximum each year into an rrsp, rather than getting paid with a dividend.

You do this because the combined rate of federal and provincial tax on corporate profits in most of the country is above 20 percent—in Ontario, for example, it's 22 percent. But in provinces with very low corporate tax rates, like Alberta and Quebec, then the reverse is true, and you should go for dividends. In general, it's a good idea to take as much money out of your company as you can, to the point where the tax you're going to pay equals what the corporation would have paid if you hadn't taken the salary. If this straps the company for cash, you can always just lend it back. Then it becomes a shareholder's loan, and the company can give it back to you at any point, free of tax.

If you're lucky enough to have a company doing over $200,000 a year, then the corporate tax rate is more than 10 percent higher. To keep the company's tax profile down, it's a good idea to take a salary equal to the amount above $200,000. If the company is taxed and then gives you a dividend—on which you have to pay tax—the feds are getting more than their pound of flesh. If you had a company doing $250,000, you would actually be $8,000 better off by taking a personal salary of $50,000. And, of course—more than ever—you need an accountant to hold your hand and guide you through this maze.

Another thought: If the company owes you money, consider charging it interest. The payments can be treated as a business expense and used as a deduction. And payments only have to be made every two years, which means you can defer taxes for that long. You pay personal tax on this income only when you receive it.

•Well, all this just forms phase one of tax reform. The second shoe has yet to drop, and when it does the sound could be deafening. Ottawa has plans to implement a national, broad-based, multistage sales tax. In effect, it will be a consumption tax. But it will also be a hidden tax.

The cost of products will be increased as they pass through the system—from raw materials to manufacturing to wholesaling, distributing and retailing. At each stage of the game, tax will be added and paid to the feds. By the time it gets to the consumer a significant portion of the purchase price will be tax, but you and the retailer and everybody else up the chain probably won't know how much.

In effect, we get taxes on taxes. Bottom-line consumer prices will rise as a result. How much is just a guess now. The feds are talking to the provinces about ways this new tax can be combined with existing provincial sales taxes so that a single, simpler charge can be levied. About all we know at this point is that the June 18 White Paper on tax reform mused over the figure of 8 percent. And after Mike Wilson told us, late in 1987, that food and drugs would be exempt from the consumption tax, he also said this would likely push the rat up by 1.5 percent or so.

We could, then, be looking at a rate of over 9 percent—and then there are provincial taxes to work in. Ontario, for example, now charges 7 percent on most retail purchases. So could consumers actually be facing a charge of 16 percent or more after phase two of tax reform clicks in?

They sure could. Ottawa plans to scrap the existing manufacturers' sales tax and replace it with the new one. At first it will just replace the lost revenue, but after that the feds hope it will be a money machine. Once in place, all they have to do is quietly raise the effective tax rate a half point or so, and raise billions more. It will be a lot less messy than having to stand up on budget night and announce new personal taxes. European countries, like Britain, have found that a tax like this is a regular cash cow.

But the problem remains that it's inflationary as hell. This tax will be applied to just about everything you buy, except food and drugs. It will also cover services you hire—like getting your hair done, or being counselled by a lawyer or accountant, or hiring a landscaper or housepainter or maid service. Everything. Because the feds warn that any exemptions from the tax will simply push the rate higher on everything else.

Let's look for a moment at what this might do to one of my favorite investments: Real estate. First, virtually all land transactions will be subject to the tax. Assume that a farmer sells raw land to a developer, who then sells it to a homebuilder, who builds and then sells the lot and house to a homebuyer. This example is prepared by the accounting firm of Peat Marwick, and it is blood-curdling, and it assumes a tax rate of 8 percent.

The farmer sells to the developer for $100,000, and there is tax payable of $8,000. The developer hands over a cheque for $108,000, and the farmer is supposed to sent eight grand to Ottawa. (Let's make it clear that this is tax on nothing. No jobs have been created. No product has been manufactured. And the buyer is also liable for provincial land transfer tax. Yetch.) Now the developer services the land and sells it to a homebuilder for $250,000. The tax now charged is $20,000. It has cost the developer $54,000 to service the land, on which he paid a tax of $4,000. So, from the $20,000 now charged there is a credit of $12,000 for tax the farmer and developer have already paid. You're still with me, I hope ...

Now a nice house is built, and it sells for $600,000. The tax payable by the purchaser is a stunning $48,000. The homebuilder remits $12,000 of this to the feds, because he'd got a credit for tax already paid—by the farmer, by the developer and by him for the cost of materials and labor (both subject to the new tax).

In the end, the cost of the house has risen by $48,000, and that is the absolute increase the consumer must fork out. The buyer does not get a credit on this tax, because he's the end user. The cost of the house has inflated by 8 percent, and the federal government has received, bit by bit, $8,000 (from the farmer), $4,000 (from the seller of servicing materials), $8,000 (from the developer), $6,000 (from the vendor of construction materials), $10,000 (from subcontractors), and $12,000 (from the homebuilder).

Now, friends, tell me how this will not be one of the most inflationary taxes in Canadian history. It will make housing even more unaffordable, and it will nail an industry already sensitive to economic trends. This is dangerous stuff—and it is being actively considered by the feds, *and they are going to do it*.

This is exactly what hundreds of thousands of Japanese marched in the streets about, enough of them that together they were able to pressure the government into changing its mind.

The average Canadian doesn't have the foggiest idea of what a multistage national sales tax will do, even though it is one of the most far-reaching structural changes ever to hit this country. Will a tax on consumption dampen consumer spending? Exactly how inflationary is it going to be? What will be the costs to everyone in the business chain of collecting all this money at all these points? What's it going to cost the government to administer and enforce a multistage sales tax? And how do we compensate for driving up the cost of basic commodities like housing?

The existing tax system is riddled with inequities. We are absurd enough, for example, to generally tax domestic products at a higher rate than imports. The current manufacturers' sales tax set-up is inherently unfair and cries out for reform. I know all this, and I know that simply throwing it out and replacing it with a national sales tax would solve a lot of problems.

But the dangers here are real, and they are not being talked about. It's time that changed, don't you think? Tell your member of Parliament, before it is too late. Any new national sales tax must be ushered in gradually. Hitting the system with 8 or 9 percent overnight, charged on virtually every item, would be a sincere shock. Canada is very much at risk.

- Here are some contacts for getting more information on tax reform:
- First, you might as well find out what the official party line is. The White Paper on tax reform, along with all the booklets that accompanied it originally, will give you the philosophy behind reform. Some of the technical details have changed—for example, in December of 1987 changes were made to the taxation of car expenses and families—but most of what's here is now law. For your copy write: Distribution Centre, Department of Finance, Ottawa, Ont. K1A 0G5 (613) or call: 995-2855.
- The accounting firm of Peat Marwick has put out two comprehensive and pretty understandable tax reform volumes. The first, *Analysis & Commentary*, is about phase one. It's 133 pages long and designed for easy reference. The second volume, *Multi-Stage Sales Tax* is an 87-page booklet about phase two. It spells out all the implications of the new consumption tax, and is an eye-opener.

  Peat Marwick, bless their little accounting hearts, has been giving away these books to people who have taken the time to ask. Check the back of this book for a list of their addresses across Canada.
- One of the first complete books on tax reform was written by a clutch of people at the accounting firm of Deloitte, Haskins & Sells; the editor was national tax director William Strain. It's called *Tax*

Reform 87—Your Guide for Personal and Business Planning. Published by Key Porter books, it's 148 pages long and sells for $6.95. I think it's worth buying.

The book is available through bookstores, or from a D. H & S office near you. Contact names and phone numbers are listed at the back of this book.

- Dunwoody and Company is another accounting firm that has pubished a worthwhile booklet on tax reform. Its "tax reform edition" of *Personal Tax Planning* is a 72-page guide to the new rules. I like the way it's laid out—the use of boxes and color helps to highlight changes and make the whole subject more understandable. Also particularly helpful is a worksheet that will help you estimate 1988 taxes when all the rules have changed. For a free copy, you can write or call: National Office, Dunwoody and Company, Royal Bank Plaza, Box 32, Toronto, Ont. M5J 2J8; (416) 865-0111. Or contact any one of their thirty-one offices throughout the country.
- Yet another big accounting firm, Coopers & Lybrand, has teamed up with the law firm of Fraser and Beatty to produce *Tax Reform '87—Analysis*, likely the most comprehensive review of tax reform that I've seen so far. Written by (count 'em) thirty-four people, and almost 200 pages long, it may be a little bookish for the average guy, but if you happen to be a professional in accounting, tax law or a related field, this is right up your alley. The publisher is CCH Canadian Limited, one of the giants in legal publishing. You can get a copy ($12.95) by writing: CCH Canadian Limited 6 Garamond Court, Don Mills, Ont. M3C 9Z9.
- There were several changes—mostly tinkering—made to the tax reform package in the dying hours of 1987, and partially as a result of the report of the House of Commons finance committee. These were some of the highlights:
- The sales tax on booze and tobacco jumped by 3 percent, to 18 percent.
- The refundable tax credit was increased by $35 to $559 a kid.
- The dependent child tax credit was hiked to $130, from the third urchin on.
- Kids under eighteen can earn up to $2,500.
- The spouse with the higher income must include family allowance payments as income, which increases the tax paid.
- People driving over 24 000 km a year on business can claim fixed and operating costs of the car.

Updates on these and other changes are available from several of the companies I mentioned above. For example, here are three I recommend:

- "Tax Reform—Full Speed Ahead," published by Deloitte, Haskins & Sells. A concise four-page update, free for the asking.
- "Tax Reform: The Next Step" is the December 16 edition of Peat Marwick's *Canadian Tax Letter*. A very comprehensive eighteen-page booklet that also gives an excellent update to the *Analysis and Commentary* book I recommended a few pages ago. Also, it's free.
- Clarkson Gordon, another national firm, has published a couple of booklets called "Stage One of Tax Reform in Canada." The first came out after the White Paper was released, and the second after the final changes were made. The second is sixteen pages long, informative and free for the asking. Ask for a copy from the company's national headquarters: Box 251, Toronto-Dominion Centre, Toronto, Ont. M5K 1J7. Or call: (416) 864-1234.

Chapter Seven

Tales from the real world

During the 1982 recession I started a newsletter for regular folks. *The Survival Letter* was as good, and cheap, as I could make it, and was intended to give out readable information on how people could weather those rough economic times.

As things turned out, times didn't get any less confusing, and the whole damn decade has been just one bang after another. The themes I've been talking about in this book have made these interesting years to live through. My newsletter has maintained its audience and found thousands of new subscribers in recent years. Increasingly I find that Canadians want in-depth but understandable information on what to do with their wealth—how to maintain what they've got, how to get more. In general, these are middle-class folks who are trying to get ahead or to achieve a certain personal target. Some of my subscribers are rich—one man earned a $1-million bonus last year—but most of them are not.

Each issue of *The Survival Letter* has responded directly to subscribers' problems. Every letter that comes in is answered and, to the best of my ability, I try to help people. Perhaps some of the following situations are like yours, and perhaps my answers can help you, too.

My wife and I own a $190,000 home, with $18,000 left on the mortgage. The mortgage is open for a few more months, at 9.5 percent. We're in the process of negotiating a private loan, however, at 7 or 8 percent from a friend to pay off the mortgage. We also have debts of $5,000 at 10.5 percent, but will discharge this loan in the next three months or sooner.

No other debts exist except on our credit cards, but these are paid off as they come due. Both of us are employed full-time, and we operate a business at home. We maximize our allowed contributions to our RRSPS.

Our monthly combined take-home pay is approximately $5,600, which consists of about $1,000 from my wife, $1,600 base pay and $3,000 in commissions from my employment. We also realize $100 to $150 in commission sales from our business as a broker/distributor. We own an old car and wonder if it can be leased legally to our company.

Our plans include leasing a new car until the end of the year and then buying it. We're also considering buying a second house for rent, or any other investment property; investing in blue chip stocks to a maximum of $10,000; or buying U.S. dollars. These ideas, however, are to be financed on borrowed funds. Your input is much appreciated.

A.V.
Scarborough, Ont.

Depending on how you look at it, you could be doing well, or you might be in for some financially rough sailing. Your combined take-home family income of over $67,000 a year is solid, but what do you have to show for it?

Besides the equity in your house, you appear to have no savings other than in your RRSP or, in fact, any other assets. With your income level, you should have enough cash around to easily discharge that mortgage, instead of simply replacing it with one at a slightly reduced rate. You should also have some money to consider a more diversified portfolio.

So where does it go? Lifestyle expenditures? It sure doesn't seem to be on investments.

By all means minimize the cost of your mortgage. And by all means lease a new car to your company (I hope it's incorporated). In fact, make liberal use of your company to provide you with as many services as possible. Could any of your commissions or bonuses be made payable to your company? Talk to your employer—it could make the difference between a tax rate of 40 percent and one of just over 20 percent.

As for your investment strategy, you can borrow against the equity in your house to invest in something else. If that something else is income-producing, then you can deduct the interest on your borrowing from your taxable income. That investment could be a house you're renting out, but I'd caution against it. The local real estate market is overvalued and could suffer a reversal within the next six months. [It did.] For that reason having all your wealth tied up in your principal residence is not the best of situations.

Besides that, rent controls and new legislation make it very unattractive to have residential rental property. It could be impossible for you to turf out tenants in the future, or to easily sell the house. If you want real estate, better that you invest in commercial, office or industrial space.

Don't even contemplate buying U.S. dollars. They are now trading at a forty-year low against the Japanese yen, and things will get worse. [They did.] America and its currency will come back, but it's going to be another couple of years. The stock market also in the opinion of many is overvalued. It has wavered on fears of interest rate increases and further dollar declines. Third World debt defaults will slap bank stocks and help fuel market nervousness.

A better bet in the short term would perhaps be gold or silver. But because precious metals don't produce income, you can't claim the interest on any money borrowed to buy them.

So the bottom line is this: Examine where your cash is going. Do a budget and strike a savings plan. Don't take on more debt right now to finance an investment. Better that you do this out of your own cash flow, after you trash the mortgage.

Can a person open a bank account in the U.S. by mail? If so, do you have the name and address of one bank, and should the account be in U.S. dollars?

J.R.
Aylmer, Ont.

Yes, you can do it by mail at most large banks (Chase Manhattan, Citibank, etc.) but I have an easier way for you. One of the most popular border banks for Canadians is Goldome, formerly the Buffalo Savings Bank. A big feature is sheer convenience.

Goldome operates a telephone service called Quick Line. You merely need to call and then open a bank account on the phone. They'll prepare whatever papers are necessary and then mail them to you. And they are used to dealing with Canadians.

Make sure you sign the "non-resident

alien" form, and the U.S. Internal Revenue Service will not withhold tax from the interest you earn. In fact, if you choose to be a tax evader, all the interest earned on that account can be yours—because the interest is not reported to Revenue Canada.

Now that federal tax reform in Canada makes every dollar of interest earned subject to tax, the idea of escaping to an American bank is enticing more and more people. You'll find that U.S. banks don't offer Canadian-dollar accounts, the way ones here deal in American currency. So you don't have a choice on that matter. And in terms of accounts, go for a CD—certificate of deposit. They pay the best interest, and the bank will just roll the funds over into a new CD when one expires—meaning you are spared the bother.

Goldome's Quick Line number in Buffalo is: (716) 847-5945.

A few weeks ago you commented that profits from the sale of rental properties did not qualify for capital gains tax exemption. I am not clear whether this referred to short-term "flips" only or to all sales of rental property. My wife and I bought our first new house in 1966 and lived in it until 1970. We then moved to our present home and rented out the previous one, which we are selling this year. Will this sale qualify for the $100,000 capital gains tax exemption?

A.W.
Toronto

You are not alone. Most small-time real estate investors believe that the money they make on property is considered a capital gain and therefore qualifies for the current exemption. In fact, the belief has been reinforced by groups as influential as Hume Publishing, which sells a national real estate investing course.

But that just isn't the case. Revenue Canada has been treating this profit as regular income rather than capital gain. Sometimes they've been doing it aggressively. Following the Vancouver real estate boom in the late 1970s, Revenue cops moved in, researched land transfers and started sending out tax bills. The profits that investors had made were clearly treated as if they were regular income.

The difference is important. With a capital gain you get to keep one-half the profit and pay tax on the other half, according to your personal tax rate. With the current exemption in place, you can realize $100,000 worth of gain and pay no tax on it. But when a profit is taxed as regular income, all of it is subject to tax, payable at your regular rate. And there is no exemption. It means someone making $30,000 on a real estate deal is liable for around $10,000 in tax. If you've not been expecting to pay any, that could come as a massive shock to your system.

In your case, it might be possible to escape this problem, primarily because of the length of time the investment has been held. Clearly the real estate was purchased as a long-term proposition and served for a while as your principal residence. I'd recommend that when you report the sale on your tax return, you do it as a capital gain. If Revenue Canada decides to reassess you, file a Notice of Objection and take the issue to tax court. You have a good chance of winning.

For others who have flipped houses, sold offers to purchase or moved in and out of real estate in a relatively short time, the prospects are not so good. There is no evidence yet that authorities have started to sift through land registry files, but such action could be just around the corner.

My late husband left me a fair sum of money,

which I transferred to a T-bill account with Canada Trust. This was just over a year ago and I still haven't moved the money around. I am wondering about buying another house and renting it, or splitting the money between the T-bill account and term deposits. Also, the rate of interest for this T-bill account is 8.25 percent. Is this the best deal as far as interest is concerned?

My late husband did all the financial planning, so I am having a hard time making decisions in this category. At present I am not employed, after working for twenty years. I decided to take a few months off to try and replan my future, but I lack financial knowledge.

M.L.
Orangeville, Ont.

In your position the most important thing is to guard the security of your money and to make sure you have a stable, adequate cash flow. Right now your capital is merely on hold.

Canada Trust's T-bill account really has nothing to do with T-bills. Real Treasury bills are purchased from investment dealers—they are usually available in denominations from $10,000 up; they are 100 percent secure; they pay more interest than Canada Trust does; and you can lock in for periods as short as ninety days. This would be a good place for a portion of your money, especially at a time when interest rates are inching higher. Contact an investment dealer and make some enquiries about purchasing some T-bills. It could be an excellent temporary solution to your problems.

Also consider investing in mortgages. There are two easy ways of doing this. From time to time issues of Cannie Maes come on the market. This is the nickname for mortgage-backed securities, or MBSS. Banks will take a mortgage portfolio and have a brokerage house issue a type of bond that is backed by these residential loans. The beauty of it is that investors receive regular monthly cheques, which would be ideal in your case. As well, the rate of interest is much higher than you're presently receiving.

Or you could invest in a mortgage fund. The Bank of Montreal's First Canadian Mortgage Fund is safe, accessible and has paid investors a high rate of return. And Royal Trust offers a DGIC—diversified guaranteed investment certificate. Three-quarters of your money is put into a high-yielding GIC and the rest goes into a mortgage fund which also pays a high rate of return.

I'd caution against rental real estate right now. Being a landlord can be a drag, and maintaining another house can cost a lot of money. Meanwhile, rents are hardly high enough now to offset the growing cost of purchasing property.

Better that you diversify in other ways—spreading your money between Treasury bills and mortgage-backed investments, which will ensure you a steady and uninterrupted flow of cash.

My husband and I live in Markham, Ontario, and own a $329,000 home which has an $80,000 mortgage. We have an in-law apartment which rents for $700 a month. Our problem: In April of 1987, when things were going great with the economy, we bought another house, in Unionville, with the intention of flipping it.

The market took a dive about a month after we bought. We have already put the required $30,000 into our new home in Unionville, which will be ready in April 1988. We want to keep both houses for investment purposes, but do you think we can? If so, how can we go about doing that? I know we can keep the one we live *in, no problem, but is it financially possible to hang on to the new one?*

Our other assets are twenty ounces of gold, $10,000 in savings bonds, $6,000 in an RRSP, $5,000 cash and a $30,000 property in New Brunswick. Our combined income is $78,000 a year, and we have $8,400 in rental income.

S.L.
Markham, Ont.

In our phone conversation after I received this letter, you gave me the missing link: the price of the property you bought in Unionville. And, at $345,000, it isn't exactly the cheapest house in town. You have chosen to make an investment in one of the most expensive, yuppie-infested near-suburbs of Toronto. Homes there run an average of $100,000 more than the average Metro-area new house price of roughly $240,000. Now, let me put it to you straight: You have a problem.

Buying a piece of single-family residential real estate in that price range is dumb. Despite a shortage of rental housing, it will be impossible to get more than $2,000 a month in rental income. Local zoning laws prevent you from parcelling the property up and creating several units in it. This means that you will have to invest over $150,000 cash into this property in order to get a positive monthly cash flow. But at that point the annual return on your investment will be virtually nil.

That means this is a lousy investment. There are lots of other places in the real estate market where a cash investment like that could yield you a very positive return. Meanwhile the market for these kinds of homes has softened in the short term. Continuing stock market uncertainty, currency fluctuations and lousy political leadership are making potential buyers think twice about jumping into up-market housing. As confidence returns, this will change.

The bottom line, anyway, is that you don't have enough cash to close the deal—not unless you draw on the equity in your principal residence by taking out another mortgage on it. And this is not something I'd recommend. In fact, you will be taking a big risk if you do. And each month you will likely see more of your wealth drained away. So start taking action now to get out of this mess.

You should list both houses for sale. Put yours out as a regular listing and offer the agreement of purchase on the Unionville property for sale. This is now commonly done, and you might find a buyer for it before construction is finished. Then simply co-ordinate the two closing dates—yours and the new buyer's—for the same day.

But face it, the chances of that happening by early April are slim. It is currently taking at least sixty days to move similar properties, and then there is a period before the deal's consummated. So you may have better luck bailing out of the Markham property. A finished house in an established area always attracts more buyers. You must be prepared to move—it's better than trying to come up with money you don't have to buy something that will be a long-term financial drag.

In either case, brace yourself for a loss. Selling either home will cost you close to $20,000 in real estate and legal fees. You also have land transfer tax to pay if the Unionville deal closes, and there will be more costs involved in discharging the old mortgage while arranging the new one. Sorry, but I'm afraid you got caught in the wringer this time. Don't put off corrective action a single day!

I share your view in the potential for capital gains in precious metals over the next few years, and I would like to participate in this market. I am thirty-one years old and fully understand the risk and rewards of trading in the futures market. I am willing to speculate $10,000 and accept the risk, to be able to participate in this leverage.

Do you feel that $10,000 is large enough to speculate this way? I am interested in the silver market, as I feel it may present a greater possible percentage return than gold. In a recent newsletter you stated that silver may purge out at about $5/oz. But while gold has just cracked the $500/oz. level (Dec.,1987), silver doesn't appear to be dropping. Would it be smart to wait a few months and, if so, are there any prices that would indicate a breakout level?

M.D.
Brantford, Ont.

Well, ten thousand bucks is plenty to get yourself into the futures market. Any broker will be more than happy to see you walk in with that kind of money. Just make sure you know that the ten grand can turn into $50,000, or it can end up costing several thousand dollars in absolute losses. Silver, meanwhile, is a very uncertain metal.

If the economic signs continue to point toward a recession, then silver prices will fall. It is considered an industrial metal and is not like gold—where nervous money flows from troubled paper investments. Five-dollar silver is still quite possible if the economy slumps. And you should note that silver has not kept pace with gold's recent advances. So the best advice at this point would be to wait and see what develops next. As silver declines, it represents more of a buying opportunity—but in the long term.

The next bull economic cycle will probably be in the early 1990s. It will also be pretty inflationary and led by rising commodity prices. At that time, silver could explode in value. Some analysts are telling me they think $50/oz. U.S. is possible. The last time that happened was when the Texas-based Hunt brothers tried to corner the market—and damn near succeeded. So it's all a matter of timing. For now, keep your powder dry, okay?

Acquaintances of ours have moved to Florida permanently with resident alien status. They will pay income tax to the U.S. We always thought it would be wonderful to retire to Florida, but have been told we must spend six months plus a day in Canada each year in order to continue receiving Canada Pension, the old age supplement and OHIP (Ontario Health Insurance Plan).

Are our friends giving up these benefits in order to live permanently in the sunny south? We will soon reach retirement age and wish we knew if becoming a resident alien in the U.S. would be a smart move—but their health care costs are appalling and we couldn't give up OHIP.

A.W.
Sarnia, Ont.

The dream of Florida retirement may be warming, but there is something of a price to pay. Canada and the U.S. penned a new tax treaty early in 1985, partly in an effort to end confusion about where taxes should be paid. The accord stipulates in general that anybody spending more than a year in the U.S. is going to be taxed there.

There are exceptions, but while a Canadian businessman looking after a U.S. operation for months on end might escape, somebody moving south full-time won't. So your resident alien friends will be treated as Americans for tax purposes.

However, they'll continue to receive CPP benefits—because those are paid to Canadian citizens no matter where they live (unfortunately in Canadian dollars). Ditto with the old age cheques, providing the recipients lived twenty years in Canada after the age of eighteen.

However, OHIP is another thing altogether. Ontario will not cover medical bills incurred by former residents who now live outside the province. You're on your own, in other words. But coverage can be resumed when a person returns to Ontario. The answer, in that case, is to have a slow illness rather than a quick accident—and lots of U.S. medical insurance in case you don't.

By the way, the best book on this subject is *How to Invest and Retire Successfully in Florida*. It's a guidebook for Canadians, written by community college professor Sidney Kling. Originally published in 1982, the book was updated and reissued in 1987 by Stoddart Publishing. Kling goes through U.S. immigration laws, health plans and investing in real estate in Florida and other Sun Belt states. At $15.95, it's worth acquiring.

After reading an article on Alberta real estate, I became very interested in revenue properties out west. Unfortunately I am not very familiar with the real estate market in western Canada. How should I concentrate my investments in real estate in Alberta?

You mentioned that condo apartments could be bought for less than $20,000. I read recently that bargains could be had in the downtown Edmonton apartment condominium market since prices have dropped substantially from peak levels five years ago. Is this one of the best real estate investments for future appreciation when the market recovers? On the other hand, what about the other types of real estate to choose from, like duplexes, triplexes or townhouses?

Recently I have been studying maps of the area, magazines about Alberta and real estate sections of Edmonton and Calgary newspapers. I plan to contact several real estate agents in the area and have them send me off a number of active listings. I don't have a lot of cash for a downpayment since my wife and I bought a house in the Montreal area. But, like you, I feel now is the right time to buy properties out west. Is this still possible with nothing down, by assuming an existing mortgage and having the owner finance the balance with a vendor take-back mortgage, and still end up with a positive cash flow?

Also, since I could only visit the properties once or twice a year, I would need a low-maintenance building. Do I need to hire a property management company? My goal is to have a net worth of a million dollars within ten years by investing in real estate. I feel this can be done by purchasing between $200,000 and $300,000 worth of real estate a year, assuming an average rate of increase of 10 percent. In any event, I believe, as you do, that prices out west are undervalued, making it bargain real estate. I am very enthusiastic, but want to be cautious so I can maximize profits and avoid hassles.

G.C.
Pincourt, Que.

Enthusiasm is a good tool to start with, but make sure you go into a western real estate investment with all the facts needed. The price of housing in cities like Edmonton is still at bargain levels, compared with much of eastern Canada. While there's been some improvement lately, values have a long way to travel to meet boom conditions of the 1970s.

Fuelling the improvement will be investor confidence as the price of a barrel of oil rises. But the return to economic health across the west has been slow, as the country's heart continues to beat in southern Ontario. The population migration has been continuing as people and money flows to job-rich Ontario. So, in the meantime, opportunity exists for real estate investors.

One of the best things about Alberta is the absence of rent controls. This means rents are set in the free market, and landlords who want to change tenants are able to do so. Higher rents mean a greater chance of buying properties with little down and getting a positive monthly cash flow. Condo prices are depressed in Edmonton because the rental vacancy rate is relatively high. But they do represent good value, because the city does not face the same future glut of units as Toronto does. The situation is even better for investors in Calgary.

Other forms of real estate will likely appreciate at a faster annual rate, with single-family detached dwellings leading the pack. As in almost every city, a duplex or triplex often offers the best positive cash flows. A building with three units or more in it also gives you the opportunity of offering accommodation to a tenant in return for maintenance duties. That helps keep up the value of your investment and provides a front-line defence against landlord-related problems.

Be careful with leveraging yourself too much. Long-distance real estate buys cost in commission, increased legal fees and travel expenses. It is really not possible to buy with "nothing" down—but by asking for vendor take-back financing, you can secure a deal with relatively little. And, yes, there are quite a few properties on the western market that allow you to put out small amounts, assuming a mortgage and securing a positive cash flow.

Your ten-year plan sounds a tad optimistic. If you buy $200,000 or $300,000 worth of real estate a year I guarantee you'll have $1 million in equity within a decade. You could also have $2 million worth of debt. Prepare yourself for that reality. It's important that you think about cash flow as well as appraised value. Buy real estate that gives you a steady income with which you can invest again or pay down existing obligations. Just amassing a string of properties can turn out to be as much a liability as an asset.

By the way, there are a great many undervalued properties in the Montreal area. Why not do more investing where you know the market better? The grass isn't always greener ...

I am going to buy a Ford pickup truck, which is going to cost approximately $21,000. I have about $32,000 in savings, which I've been thinking about putting into a GIC and collecting 9.25 percent or more.

I want to find out how to borrow. What's the best way to purchase this truck? I'd rather keep my money in a GIC than pay cash for the vehicle. I am able to pay about $900 a month on a loan.

H.P.
Scarborough, Ont.

Okay, this is the rule of thumb I always follow: You use your money to buy things that appreciate, and you rent the things you need but which depreciate. Cars and trucks are classic examples. The depreciation factor is great, and it's almost unavoidable. Right now only some vintage cars—and just about every Ferrari ever built—steadily increase in value.

So there's a powerful argument for leasing vehicles and buying real estate. If you now rent real estate and make a habit of buying trucks, then you'd better get used to not being rich. Leasing plans have become vastly more flexible and affordable in the past few years. I'd suggest you look into it—making sure you have a reasonable pay-out at the end of the lease, and no mileage limits.

If you do want the pickup, then buy it with cash. Then take out a loan and invest the money in a money market mutual fund. You'll earn at least 8 percent, and the interest on your loan will be tax deductible. Or, if you don't like that, you could buy the truck using a bank personal line of credit. You can repay the loan as fast as you want, and if your credit's good, you'll probably get a better rate.

But there's something else to consider here: Because of tax reform, all the interest on the GIC you're contemplating is taxable, now that the $1,000-a-year deduction is gone. That drastically reduces the real return your money earns. In terms of purchasing power, you'd be going nowhere. The gain you'd make over inflation is eaten away by tax. So consider investing in something that can yield a tax-free capital gain, like precious metals or a principal residence, where profits are still tax-free.

Finally, a $21,000 Ford pickup? A new Ford F150 can be had for about $11,000—and keeps a respectable part of its value. It must take a lot of shopping to be able to spend almost twice that much on a variation of the same vehicle. Don't buy more truck than you need.

My mortgage is $70,000 at 11 percent, with an annual prepayment privilege of 10 percent. The amortization is twenty-five years and the term expires in 1991. I looked around at mortgages and found one for three years at 11 percent, also with a 10 percent annual prepayment. It can be paid weekly, and has the option to double payments—also on a twenty-five-year amortization.

My monthly income tells me I could double my payments and also pay that 10 percent a year on the principal. Would it be worth paying a $1,900 penalty to cancel or pay off my old mortgage? And how soon could I pay my $70,000 debt, with the mortgage I'd like to switch to?

L.L.
Pickering, Ont.

Now don't get too restless—you aren't as badly off as you might think. Your mortgage is actually very competitive in terms of rates. And I think you are underestimating the pay-out penalty. In times of rising rates, you will have to pay three months' payments or the difference between your rate and current rates over the balance of your loan—whichever is greater.

Some lenders, in fact, charge you both a three-month penalty and the rate difference. Others (Barrie, Ont.–based Municipal Savings and Loan comes to mind) charge a whopping six months' payments plus the interest rate bonus. So make sure you get a pay-out commitment in writing before you consider any course of action. It would make more sense to wipe that amount off your principal than to give it to your bank.

But you are correct in being envious of a mortgage that you can pay weekly and that gives you the option of doubling up on payments. Generally speaking, by making weekly payments you can pay off a mortgage amortized over twenty-five years in just thirteen years, and save thousands in interest. Doubling payments, whether weekly or monthly, has roughly the same effect, because the amount of accruing interest is slashed.

But you don't necessarily need a bank to do that. You can embark on your own ambitous savings program between now and the time the mortgage comes due. Invest cash in something safe and liquid, which pays a decent rate of return—like T-bills. When the mortgage comes due, then slap all this cash against it. Go with a lender at that point who will give you more flexibility with payments. And reduce the amortization as far as possible. Remember: The longer it is, the lower the payments, but the greater the amount of money you have to pay back.

A $70,000 mortgage amortized over twenty-five years, without prepayments, will cost you over $210,000 in payments. So the faster you get rid of the sucker, the better. But the best bet now is to stick with your existing mortgage and save. Historically speaking, 11 percent for a five-year loan ain't bad.

I have a rock collection, which I have amassed over twenty-five years. In the collection there are substantial samples of rock bearing gold.

How do I go about extracting the gold ore from these rocks and turning it into the marketable commodity? Do I go to the same place that a gold prospector goes to? And where is that place? Or would I go to a foundry—but would the melt be pure, and therefore marketable? Could you please help me on this one, as I have assets which at the moment appear to have no value.

G.B.
Toronto

You will have to take your rocks to a recognized assayer/refiner, have them analyzed and then processed. This involves an element of risk, and expense, on your part. The refiner may not recover much gold from the rocks, while at the same time wrecking your collection.

On the other hand, you could be sitting on some valuable ore. In Toronto a good outfit is Johnson-Matthey. They say they will be happy to assay your rocks and then refine them. The initial cost of the testing will be about $50, with refining extra. The company is located at 110 Industry Road; call ahead first: (416) 763-5111.

My husband and I are fifty-eight and fifty-seven respectively. We both have decent-paying jobs and are on company pension plans. Since it is our second marriage we are, in effect, starting over. We live in an apartment (rented quite reasonably at $425 a month). My husband has an inheritance coming from Britain of between $40,000 and $50,000 (depending on the exchange rate).

I would like to buy a lot and put a Viceroy home on it in the Midland or Coldwater area, and keep within our means. Hopefully we'd have the house ready for retirement—paid for at that time, about four years from now. Meantime we would stay in our apartment and work.

My husband is leaning toward buying a home now in Toronto and moving in; then selling it in three or four years, buying a rural property and retiring. We have a lot and trailer in a condominium park worth about $25,000, which is paid for and which we would like to keep. Which is the best way to go? Is there any other alternative?

I.B.
Downsview, Ont.

One of the most important things you can do to prepare for a hassle-free retirement is to stabilize your housing costs. You can do that in several ways. Simply staying in your rent-controlled apartment is one of them—but probably the least satisfying. Of the two choices you've presented, one clearly has more potential for profit.

If you construct the retirement home when the inheritance comes through, you'll be carrying, at best, about $100,000 worth of financing (even pre-fab houses aren't cheap, once you factor in the cost of a well, septic system and foundation). Real estate values in the Midland/Coldwater area have appreciated over the years, but at a rather sluggish rate compared with Toronto. So, while you carry this home, your equity is unlikely to grow very quickly. Meanwhile you will still be responsible for your rent.

If you buy a city home, assuming $50,000 down and an average house price, then you'll be carrying about $150,000 in financing. This will just about equal the cost of mortgaging the vacation home while also paying rent on the apartment. But the value of the Toronto property will rise far more quickly, carrying your equity with it. If you hold it for four years, there's every reason to believe that prices will have escalated from the $200,000 range to around $300,000. The gain realized will also be free of taxes.

So you could come out of that experience with about $150,000 clear—which is more than enough to purchase a retirement nest. Sorry to side with your husband, but a move into fast-track urban real estate looks like the best bet.

A year ago I made a highly-leveraged purchase of a thirteen-suite apartment building. On an after-tax basis, I am just about breaking even. In a recent newspaper article a so-called market guru forecast a Depression even worse than the 1930s. How would my investment fare in a depression? Should I be thinking of unloading it?

K.A.
Calgary,. Alta.

A number of people are making headlines by calling for a big blow-out similar to that which leveled the world almost sixty years ago.

But a recession—perhaps severe, and maybe worse than the 1982 setback—is more likely. And it will probably start in late 1987 and take hold in 1988/89.

The recession will be started primarily because of the global debt crisis, and come to smash many financial markets. Stocks will be hit hard, but real estate will not be left untouched. It's reasonable to expect prices will retreat by 15 to 20 percent.

If that happens, the appraised value of your apartment building will probably fall below the mortgaged amount. In the event of a mortgage renewal, you might be in a tough situation—having to come up with a substantial chunk of cash to make up the difference.

Also in a debtbased recession it is unlikely you could ask for much in the way of additional rent to cover increased financing costs.

So, if the value of your real estate is unlikely to grow and may, in fact, fall—then you have to question the wisdom of hanging on to a breakeven property.

Maybe it's time to unload. But take your time in finding the best buyer—Calgary real estate prices have been artificially depressed and have only recently started to catch up with the rest of the country.

Try advertising this investment opportunity in a place like Toronto where property values have soared. Somebody there will be only too happy to take it off your hands.

I've invested in gold and silver and now have about $10,000 worth. I feel I should keep it because of the low price I paid, and future expectations. However, I am interested in purchasing some lakefront property in northern Ontario. The high price of property makes me wonder if I should wait for prices to decline before buying.

Should I sell my gold and silver to use as a full

downpayment, or should I keep it and buy with a small amount down? I have a small income and am in my early twenties. Any advice would be greatly appreciated.

D.B.
Brampton, Ont.

First, the metals: The behavior of gold and silver suggests that they anticipate a recession. If these days were normal, then gold prices would be exploding. After all, the U.S. buck has been in trouble, sliding to serious lows against the Japanese yen and German mark. The Iran-Iraq war continues to dominate the Persian Gulf. Stock markets have virtually bled to death, and Ronald Reagan has proven himself unable to face the perils threatening America. And yet who stronger is there to succeed him?

Under these conditions gold should be $600 U.S. an ounce, rather than being mired in the $400 trading range. Why so low? Because when there's a recession the price of commodities falls as cash becomes the most prized commodity. Gold is telling us now that there's trouble ahead. So don't sell, not when prices are far lower than they should be. Hang on, and after the recession is over, those metals will take off.

Now, on to real estate. One of the immediate results of Black Monday was a softening in parts of the "secondary" real estate market—cottages, hobby farms and other recreational properties. Resale properties in general held up fairly well. New housing sales, however, were hit hard. And for the secondary market, the future is quite clouded. Prices could soften as recessionary fears take hold. This, of course, is good news for someone in the position to buy. Bargains are likely lying ahead for those out shopping.

But do you have enough money? A downpayment of $10,000 is going to get you nowhere, not if this lakefront property is going to be worth anything, or have proper road access. Remember that the banks and trust companies give you more grief when trying to get a mortgage on a non-urban property. Many simply refuse to get involved with the recreational market. Others charge up to a half-point premium on the mortgage rate. And all of them are very reluctant to go with high-ratio financing on property like this. So make sure you have 25 percent of the price to put down before even making an offer.

And make your offer conditional upon several things: Being provided an up-to-date survey (rural properties are legendary for encroachments, unopened road allowances and the like). Also have a condition allowing you to secure satisfactory financing within ten business days. Other conditions should include a water potability test and certificate (or guarantee) that the septic conforms to all municipal requirements.

Check the well (it should be drilled) and the location of the septic bed. Go to the municipal offices and check the zoning; while you're there ask a few friendly questions, like has anyone heard of a hydro-electric corridor going through, or are the roads plowed in winter? In general, lakefront cottages have soared in value over the past few years. But, as with most real estate, the premium properties have enjoyed the best appreciation. Maybe, given your tender age, it would be a better bet to start investing with a principal residence. That way, you get to live in it year-round. It's easier to liquidate. It's more recession-proof. It's also cheaper to finance. Give it some serious thought—and save some more money.

I will be retiring this fall with a small company pension of approximately $755 a month, plus

CPP and oldage security. My RRSP is in the form of a GIC, due later this year, and has a principal of $140,010, after tax. I have another GIC worth $68,800.

I have 87 one-ounce gold wafers, and a $20,000 mortgage paying 15 percent, due in 1988. Currently I have $15,000 in the bank, paying around 6 percent. The GIC I have in a bank and the RRSP is in a trust company, but I would feel more secure having it all in banks, even knowing the deposit insurance does not cover all the accounts.

My income tax while working has been high. What changes could I make to my position to increase the return and decrease tax now and when I retire. Is the American way still a good route for the after-tax money, as I intended to purchase a trailer in Florida, anyway? What would be the best protection for the rest of my assets?

D.M.
Willowdale, Ont.

With assets of almost $300,000, excluding any real estate you may own, you're doing okay. All that's needed is some fine-tuning. Consider these points:

- The worst return you are getting is from that cash in the bank. And under tax reform, it is fully exposed to taxation now. So try to do better. It would be a good idea to withdraw most of that—leaving a little for emergencies—and put it in a Treasury bill. These will pay you about 8 percent, while being convenient, secure and liquid. Should interest rates rise, you can take advantage of that.
- I assume you have been buying gold for some time and have an average purchase price of $400 or less. If that is the case, then you should start thinking about taking some profits. Gold should start to strengthen after the recession takes hold and the economy starts looking forward to the next growth period. Sell on that strength—about 40 ounces near the $500 mark, holding the rest for longer-term appreciation.
- With the liquid assets you have now, there should be no reason to cash in the RRSP and trigger tax. Your income for this year will still be sizable, so the tax owing on the RRSP could be cut by waiting for a year in which you earn less. Roll over the retirement savings plan and make some enquiries about converting it into an annuity down the road.
- You might consider another way to increase your regular income, rather than relying solely on interest (which can be a mistake in times like these). An investment in income real estate might make a lot of sense. As real estate prices soften, investment opportunities open up. Putting money into a duplex, triplex or good commercial property could give you monthly income and tax advantages.
- Don't move your money to a U.S. bank. Conditions there have changed substantially. A record number of banks failed in 1987, and the feds are worried about many, many more. The economy there is in turmoil and the currency is under global pressure. I'd even have second thoughts about investing in a trailer, or U.S. real estate. Foreigners are subject to several taxes that Americans are not. You might be ahead of the game, and less burdened, by renting.
- Finally, keep on making RRSP contributions. Open a spousal plan, if you don't have one now. This is the most effective way you still have of reducing your tax bill. Ottawa plans to raise the maximum allowable contribution levels significantly over the next few years, and this will work directly to your benefit.

Retire in dignity. Retire in wealth.

Chapter Eight

Living the myth a little while longer

In November of 1987 the editors of *Your Money* magazine asked me to write an article on how movements in the economy affect real estate prices. Coming hard on the heels of Black Monday, it looked like the economy might nosedive into recession—but only time would tell if central bankers and politicians could keep their act together.

I agreed, and was then shocked to learn that the article would be published in April, about six months after I wrote it. Looking that far into the future seemed an impossible task.

I mention this here because, while it is essential to look down the economic road, anybody who tells you they can is either an idiot or a liar. Circumstances have been changing so quickly that long-term forecasting is nothing much more than a guess. In early 1988, for example, the chief economist at Merrill Lynch predicted a recession by the spring of 1989. Finance Minister Mike Wilson, on the other hand, has just told Canadians that 1989 will bring euphoria—including steady 3 percent economic growth, a surge in exports, inflation below 4 percent, unemployment 1 percent lower and a drop in interest rates.

Weird? You bet. But weirdness was a big part of the February 10, 1988, federal budget.

I spent that afternoon in Ottawa's National Conference Centre, in the great hall where federal-provincial meetings are held. This used to be the city's train station, and sits across the street from the soaring Chateau Laurier Hotel, just a block from Parliament Hill. The hall has a ceiling forty feet off the floor, supported by great circular pillars around the walls.

The budget lock-up that afternoon was four and a half hours long, shorter than normal—the reason being painfully obvious. Despite being in six volumes, and three hundred pages long, the budget contained virtually no news. In ten years of covering federal budgets, this was the first time I'd ever encountered anything like this. There was only one single new budget-type measure in it—a tax of 1 cent a litre on gasoline, raising a miserable $300 million a year in federal revenues.

Journalists spent a lot of time wandering around, interviewing each other and returning to the buffet lunch table. Once in, the security guards would not let you out—whether there was anything to write about or not.

"As Canadians look ahead to a new decade and a new century," the budget began, started, "they have good reason to look forward with confidence." It was hard to believe what I was reading, in the wake of Black Monday, wild currency fluctuations and mutterings about recession. But it soon became clear: the Mulroney Tories were giving up the fight.

They had decided to be political animals, telling the country that everything was splendid, the future was bright and the economy was under control. But doing this also meant turning their backs on the struggle to slash the federal deficit and contain the growing national debt. Frankly, I was shocked and deeply disappointed, because if the Tories won't face the music and be fiscally responsible, you can be damn sure the Liberals and New Democrats won't.

By week's end, even the left-leaning Toronto Star was calling for further cuts in the deficit. But Mike Wilson kept on smiling.

That budget had some disturbing assumptions at its heart. One was that the Canada-U.S. free trade pact would sail right through a protectionist American Congress and become law by 1990. Nowhere was there any hint of what economic path Ottawa would follow if the deal was turned back or altered. And then there was the belief that the economy would take a sharp turn for the better, after a modest decline in 1988. Wilson was talking about near-boom conditions at the same time others were warning that the American empire was sliding into a recession of unknown depths. Wilson used this forecast of good times that to draw a veil over the debt and the deficit. But even with his best-case scenario in place, the budget numbers themselves were chilling.

This is the latest forecast (and remember, the government bases these projections on a strong economy, low unemployment, lower rates and less inflation. Change any one of those elements, and the picture grows much darker):

In 1988 the government will spend $29 billion to pay the interest on the outstanding debt we've already run up. About $22 billion of that will be borrowed money. The government will spend $29.3 billion more this year than it will take in. That's a slight improvement from the $30.6 billion shortfall the year before—and most of that can be attributed to the new penny gas tax and a cut of $300 million in federal spending, details of which weren't even announced in the budget.

What does this mean? Simply that our debt is going to get a lot worse. Look at this chart, published by the finance department. It paints a sorry picture.

All those figures are in *billions* of dollars. This chart tells us that under the best-case conditions the following is going to happen:

Budgetary Transactions
(in billions of dollars)

	1984-5	1985-6	1986-7	1987-8	1988-9	1989-90
Revenues	70.9	76.8	85.8	96.1	103.3	106.3
Expenditures	-109.2	-111.2	-116.4	-125.3	-132.3	-134.9
Deficit	-38.3	-34.4	-30.6	-29.3	-28.9	-28.6
Financial Requirements	-29.8	-30.3	-21.6	-20.9	-22.3	-18.7
Program Expenditures	86.8	85.8	89.7	96.1	100.2	101.9
Net Public Debt	199.	233.	264.	293.	322.	351.
% of Gross Domestic Product	44.7	48.7	51.8	53.1	54.9	56.1

- The federal deficit will decline by only $700 million over the next two years—and $600 million of that will come from higher gasoline taxes.
- The feds are going to have to borrow almost $21 billion in 1988/89, another $22.3 billion the year after and almost $19 billion more after that.
- Despite this worsening situation, federal spending will continue to grow each year, experiencing 25 percent growth in a six-year period.
- Our national debt will escalate, from under $200 billion when the government took office to $293 billion in 1988, and then to $351 billion by the next fiscal year.

So what? So in 1984 it cost us $24.4 billion a year to finance the national debt. In 1988 that cost rose to $29.2 billion. By 1989/90 it will be $33 billion. That is a 50 percent increase in five years, which is not exactly the definition of good financial management. The sad part is that we are destined to have higher debt service charges one year after another. As long as the feds keep running deficits, the debt will grow.

And consider this: If we have a recession, then the burden on government will grow, and the taxes it collects will fall. Right now, with 8 percent unemployment, Ottawa spends $10.1 billion a year on unemployment insurance benefits. If the unemployment rate were to rise to 10 percent (easily achieved in a modest recession), the government would have to cough up another $3 to $4 billion. At the same time, corporate taxes would plummet, personal income taxes would be reduced, and the government could be $5 billion or more short. Suddenly, a $29 billion deficit turns into a $37 billion one—right back where we were at the end of the 1982 recession.

The likely results: a run on the Canadian dollar, and higher interest rates as the central bank tries to defend it.

Is Mike Wilson playing with fire? You bet he is. And by not working harder to chop the deficit and slow the cancerous growth of the national debt, he has helped put the country at serious risk. We were failed by the spending habits of the Trudeau Liberal years; now the Mulroney Tories appear willing to sell out the country for a second term in office.

The real tragedy here is that most Canadians do not understand the debt, the deficit, or how either impacts on their lives. No political leader has the guts to make it a public issue, to explain what has been going on, how we got here, what comes next. Instead they concentrate on spending programs, constantly promising more, whether it's a national daycare program or aid to western grain farmers.

Will it take an economic crisis to force tough political decisions? Or will we get a tough politician who will act to avoid that crisis? Or are we already too far gone?

Solving the structural problems is going to require the kind of determination Canadians aren't used to, especially when we're coming off a period of prolonged economic expansion. In January of 1988 *Maclean's* magazine published the results of its annual poll on Canadians' attitudes. The results— and the reporting—were interesting.

Almost 80 percent of respondents were satisfied with their current economic situations, and 85 percent optimistic about their prospects. In Ontario, 84 percent said they were satisfied and happy with their lives. Also worth noting—in a survey conducted just a month after Black Monday—is that the single largest group of respondents said the draft free trade agreement between Canada and the U.S. was the top economic issue facing the country.

Why didn't they choose high interest rates, unemployment, the lack of affordable housing, intense regional disparities, the threat of recession or the leapfrogging national debt? Because these are not "media" issues. The media in this country do a dismal job of explaining the economy, while they devote vast resources to the coverage of political events. Free trade is more political than it is economic. Obviously Canada benefits by having some protection against American trade barriers. But the American empire is in decline. If we continue to do 80 percent of our export business with that country, we too will also be in decline.

The Maclean's poll was also typically reported: the economy took up two pages; AIDS, sexuality and fantasies covered five.

When this is the way, Canadians can hardly be blamed for a basic ignorance of what dangers face the country. But their leaders can. When Finance Minister Mike Wilson stood to make his February budget speech, he was more than aware of the close-to-insurmountable problems in the real economy. Only days before, both the C. D. Howe Institute and the Canadian Chamber of Commerce had warned loudly that increasing spending while giving up on the deficit would have dire consequences. Though Wilson chose to ignore them, his budget documents, under the heading *"The Need for Fiscal Correction,"* spelled out the simple truth.

"Over time, rapid growth in public debt also leaves the government's fiscal position highly exposed to interest rate increases, and severely restricts the government's flexibility, as the costs of servicing the higher debt account for an increasing share of total expenditures. The stock of debt itself generates large interest payments each year, and additions to that stock through ongoing deficits add further to those payments. This year alone, public debt charges will be more than $29 billion—an amount equivalent to the deficit itself—or almost 25 per cent of total government spending. In this situation, growth of public debt charges reduces the resources available for more productive spending on programs and requires reductions in program spending or revenue increases just to keep the growth in interest payments from raising the deficit further."

But that is not what Canadians read the next day in the papers, because only Wilson's budget speech was reported. And this is what he had said:

"I believe that this generation of Canadians wants to leave our children and grandchildren a legacy of opportunities and optimism, not one of crushing debt and crushed hopes.

"Our challenge in 1984 was to restore fiscal stability and rebuild credibility in the management of government finances. The only way to do that was to set out a medium-term fiscal plan with sustained deficit reduction—and then hold to that plan.

"This is exactly what we did. We embarked on a series of actions to restore fiscal order by cutting government spending and increasing revenues."

If only that were true. In 1989, for the first time in recent history, interest payments on the outstanding debt will be greater than the current deficit. It will cost us $32 billion to finance that debt—a charge that will go higher every year in the forseeable future. In 1984 the annual bill was $22.5 billion, or 50 percent less. After almost six years of continuous economic growth, how is it that our country is $300 billion in debt, and cruelly saddled with horrendous annual payments?

The answer, simply, is that we have been

living beyond our means. And the guys we trusted to keep on top of stuff like that have abandoned us. They don't run for office to accomplish goals. Instead, they run just to win office. The power and the perks and the prestige attract them. Not the responsibility of leadership.

I tell you all this just to make you more aware of the desperate need for individual action. Any sane mind can recognize the dangers and see the inevitability of some resolution to these national problems. Will we end up like Mexico, Argentina and Brazil, countries where the standard of living has been ground into the dust as governments scramble to meet foreign debt payments? After the U.S., Canada is the most indebted nation on earth. And we no longer owe money just to ourselves—we owe hundreds of billions to foreigners, who are not interested in your standard of living. Instead, they want your cash, year after year after year.

In Canada in the late 1980s, individuals have to do what the state cannot. They have to shun debt, build equity and try to isolate themselves from the reckoning. It may not happen with the next government, but surely the one after. Some internal economic upheaval will underscore the need for dramatic action. Government spending will have to be slashed, not just trimmed. The quality of services will decline, personal tax burdens will rise even further, the security of an oldage pension will be shattered. Suddenly Maclean's polls will show middle-income Canadians are less concerned with sexual fantasies and more concerned with personal financial survival.

If you don't agree that this will happen, then don't worry about it. Go on demanding that government provide cradle-to-grave social services. Elect politicians who promise to spend rather than save. Consider the country to be made up of fund-seeking special interest groups rather than a people with common goals. Do what you have been doing.

But if you can see a glimmer of truth in these words, then set a new course. Follow some of the guidelines in this book to gather together, then protect, your wealth. Stabilize your housing costs. Be an aggressive, yet cautious, investor. Plan your own business future. Take advantage of obvious buying opportunities. Pay down debt. Do not make excessive use of leveraging. Invest, don't spend. Buy assets that appreciate, rent those that don't. Work for your future, and don't expect to be taken care of.

I know this is a message a great many Canadians do not want to hear, especially in my own generation. We—the Baby Boomers, the yuppies—are supposed epitomize consumerism. Sadly, many of us do. We get bigger mortgages so we can buy all new appliances. We don't bother bargaining, haggling or negotiating, in case that indicates we don't have unlimited funds. We vacation as if it's a national right. We wear and drive and live in our wealth rather than banking or investing it. We are slaves to social trends and miss seeing the larger economic ones. In 1930 public figures like Michael Wilson were telling society that all was well. Those who believed it and continued with their old lifestyles ended up broken. Those who conserved cash, cut spending and reduced costs were the ones who scored. When the Depression hit and real estate crashed, they were the ones out snapping up bargains.

I'm not saying this is the equivalent of 1930, or that a Depression is coming. But it is obvious to those who look up that the economy as we know it is unsustainable. The myth can be lived out for a while longer, but unless action is taken soon against the debt/deficit monster, the fall will inevitably be worse.

Survival in this world, then, lies in your own hands. You can consume and run with the crowd. Or you can set your own course and get comfortable with independence.

As far as I'm concerned, there is no choice.

Good luck to us all.

Chapter Nine

There's no reason we have to part now

I started out my professional life as a journalist. Then I went into business, back into journalism, and now I practice a delicate blend of the two. Years ago I was a reporter. More lately I have come to not just report, but to interpret. And helping people has given me the kind of satisfaction an ambulance-chasing reporter never tastes.

On dozens of occasions I've received letters from people thanking me for doing something as simple as pointing out to them how enslaving their mortgages were. They took my advice, started shorting amortizations or going with weekly payments or making prepayments - and were shocked that the loan could be paid back so fast, or that personal cash flow would be so much better as a result.

I like getting those letters, or taking phone calls from people who think a little information has just brightened up a lot of their financial life. Canadians are smart people. They are diligent, hard-working and aggressive. But too often middle-class people succeed in spite of themselves. They get by when they could get rich. They continue to work as employees all of their lives when they could be working for themselves. They make after-tax payments on loans when they could be writing off the interest. They miss opportunities.

A lot of this has to do with the fact our school system traditionally didn't teach you how to handle money. How to make white sauce and work a lathe? Sure. But not how to survive in the real world. Often I'm asked to give investment seminars to professional groups - and you wouldn't believe the number of teachers I run across who are absolute babes in the fianncial woods. The middle class in this country is so busy going to work that it doesn't take the time to learn the shortcuts to wealth.

Seven years ago I decided to try and produce a regular monthly update on investment opportunities, the economy and strategies for personal success. *The Survival Letter* was the result. It started with a few dozen people who wanted to see a way out of the misery of the 1982 recession. Then a few hundred, and today several thousand.

There are a number of people in this country who set themselves up as financial advisors, usually running newspaper ads for free seminars. I know some of these people, and there are none that I respect professionally. They are, without exception, selling something. Usually it's shares in mutual funds - a lot of them high-commission, high-risk turkeys. With some others it's a course, in no-money-down real estate or starting a small business. These courses are fabulously expensive and the information you receive could have come from a thirteen-buck book like this one.

There are also some other newsletters selling financial advice. At least one is entirely written by people who are selling financial services - a stockbroker, an insurance agent, a fund salesman and so on.

What they say is presented as impartial financial advice - which is a horrible trick to play on unsuspecting subscribers.

I wanted to do something different. I wanted to see if there was a market for truthful, honest information which didn't promise to make you rich while you slept but instead set out the steady course to independence. And there was. *The Survival Letter* is published every month and it goes across the country. Just about everything recommended in the newsletter is something I have done myself or have close knowledge of. I take a lot of time getting to understand where the economy is going and what this will mean for average people. Only then, I believe, can you plot a course of action.

For somebody to tell you - day in and day out, through booms and recessions - that a single investment, like stocks or mutual funds, is the way to go is crazy. It's often a lie, but the commissions keep on getting collected.

I won't be part of that. I have been asked to speak publicly on behalf of investment companies, real estate firms, mutual funds and no-money-down real estate gurus. Every time, the answer's been no. I will speak only for myself.

For this reason *The Survival Letter* carries no advertising, and never will. It impartially tells you what new financial products are good, and which ones are a crock. No company or institution will ever see a copy of its mailing list. This publication, and another one which I began three years ago - *Real Estate Watch* - have nothing going for them other than the credibility of the words they carry. I will not tell subscribers anything that I do not believe, and I'd recommend nothing I wouldn't do myself.

The newsletters are written on tight deadlines, so the information in them is extremely up-to-date. They are mailed first-class, and arrive typically within days of leaving my office. I think it's critical in economic times like these to have the best, most time-sensitive data possible. You need to know if interest rates are going up or down, for example, when deciding between a short or long-term mortgage. You need warning of recessionary days ahead and you must be alerted to buying opportunities.

The Survival Letter is about personal financial planning. In many ways, it's like an extra chapter to this book every 30 days. The things I've talked about here are affected constantly by politics or the economy. Tax laws change. Currencies gyrate. Commodities rise and fall. Real estate gets buffeted by interest rates or consumer confidence.

In every problem, there's an opportunity. In each opportunity, some reason to be cautious. That's what *The Survival Letter* is all about. I answer all subscriber's letters, and I give my best advice based on that person's situation. I will do this as consistently, honestly and cheaply as I can.

If you have found this book of value, then stick with me and more of the same will be coming every few weeks. I am pleased to report that with the publication of the book I can offer new subscribers a break - please see the coupon printed here for details.

For those who would like to concentrate their investments in real estate (and my heart is with you), *Real Estate Watch* is devoted solely to keeping you on top of the Canadian real estate market. Each month this newsletter gives updates on mortgage products, and rates. Tips on creative financing for maximum profits. How-to articles on buying and selling. You also get in-depth coverage of the hot and cold markets, as I try to pinpoint bargains and warn of over-priced situations.

Market trends are crucial to good real estate investing, so Real Estate Watch concentrates on this area. The market is put in the context of the economy as a whole, so the effect of tax changes or interest rates or government policies can be measured. While never more exciting, real estate investing has never been so complicated, either; or more flexible, or more profitable.

A decade ago it would have been unthinkable that established mortgage brokers would offer 100% financing; that banks would have weekly-pay mortgages; or that houses could be bought and sold on the futures market, without ever taking delivery of the actual product. But all that, and much more, is taking place today. And to keep on top of an ever-changing investment scene, you need accurate, up-to-date information.

That's why I started to publish this newsletter almost three years ago. It was clear to me then that Canadian real estate was undervalued and ripe for a quick run-up. In most markets, that happened - often with a vengeance.

I don't care if you're just starting out, looking for a single good investment opportunity or adding to a big portfolio - you need accurate information to avoid making costly mistakes. It is my job to make sure both of these monthly newsletters do the job. If they don't, you get your money back. It's just that simple.

Here's how to subscribe:

1) If you live in Ontario, then simply call our toll-free telephone number. This is for *credit card orders only* - on either Visa or MasterCard - so please make sure you have your card handy when you call. By subscribing this way, we can generally have the first newsletter mailed to you within a week. Please call during regular business hours.

The number: **1-800-265-2993**

2) Or, use the coupon on the following page. I am making a special offer on both newsletters, as a thank-you for buying this book. The regular price for 12 issues of *The Survival Letter* is $49 for twelve issues. *Real Estate Watch* is $60, also for twelve issues. But, with the coupon printed here, you can get either (or both) for an extra month, for no extra money.

If you are unhappy, send the newsletter back and I'll send your money back. If you have any personal financial or investment questions, write me and - as a subscriber - you will get a response.

As a subscriber you will be offered a special deal on all future books, courses or critical material that I produce. And, as a subscriber, I think you'll be receiving the nation's most aggressive and informed financial tool. No gimmicks. No get-rich-overnight stuff. Just a steady jog on the path to independence.

I look forward to doing it with you.

PEAT MARWICK OFFICES

British Columbia

Vancouver: 2400-Royal Centre, 1055 E.Georgia St. V6E 3P3 (604) 662-5500

Richmond: No. 212-4800 No.3 Road, V6E 3P3 (604) 273-0011

Coquitlam: Heron Centre, 566 Lougheed Highway, V3K 3S3 (604) 939-1131

Prince George: 2nd Floor, Scotia Bank Bldg., 1488 Fourth Avenue, V2L 4Y2 (604) 563-7151

Abbotsford: 2309 McCallum Rd. Suite C, V2S 3N7 (604) 859-5709

Alberta

Calgary: Suite 2500, 700 Second St. S.W., T2P 2W2 (403) 267-3200

Calgary South: Suite 1000, Southland Tower, 10655 Southport Rd.S.W.
T2W 4Y1 (403) 271-9450

Edmonton: 2100 Principal Plaza, 10303 Jasper Avenue, T5J 3N6 (403) 421-4114

Fort McMurray: 200 Morrison Centre, 9914 Morrison Street, T9H 4A4 (403) 791-9000

Saskatchewan

Saskatoon: Suite 201, 500 Spadina Cr.E., S7K 4H9 (306) 652-6515

Regina: 200 Saskatchewan Place, 1870 Albert Street, S4P 4B7 (306) 757-1211

Manitoba

Winnipeg: 500-363 Broadway Avenue, R3C 3N9 (204) 949-1594

Ontario

Sault Ste. Marie: 421 Bay St., Box 368, P6A 5M1 (705) 949-3230

Windsor: 500 Canada Building, 384 Ouellette Avenue, N9A 1A8 (519) 258-8404

London: Suite 700, 200 Queens Avenue, N6A 1J3 (519) 672-47880

Waterloo: Suite 550, Allen Square, 180 King St.S., N2J 1P8 (519) 745-1500

Hamilton: One James Street South, L8P 4R5 (416) 522-9256

Burlington: 3350 South Service Rd., L7N 3M6 (416) 681-3477

Woodbridge: Suite 200, 700 Pine Valley Dr., L4L 1A8 (416) 856-5666

Toronto: Commerce Court West, King & Bay Streets, Box 31, M5L 1B2 (416) 863-3300

Markham: Suite 3, 2851 John Street, L3R 5R7 (416) 477-9140

Mississauga: Suite 1150, Two Robt. Speck Parkway, L4Z 1H8 (416) 275-6212

Ottawa: 21st Floor, Tower B, Place de Ville, 112 Kent St., K1P 5P2 (613) 237-2120

Quebec

Montreal: 1155 boul. Dorchester oeust, H3B 2J9 (514) 879-3300

Atlantic Canada

Moncton: CN Marine Bldg., 100 Cameron St., Box 827, E1C 8N6 (506) 857-8012

Halifax: Purdy's Wharf Tower, Suite 1001, 1959 Upper Water St., B3J 3N2 (902) 429-9443

St. John's: Viking Bldg., Crosbie Road, A1B 3K3 (709) 722-5593

DELOITTE, HASKINS & SELLS OFFICES

National office: Toronto: (416) 861-9700 William Strain

Prince George: (604) 564-7281 Robert McFarlane

Vancouver: (604) 669-4466 Peter Clayden

Victoria: (604) 386-2164 Steven Reed

Calgary: (403) 298-3900 Michael Lavery

Edmonton: (403) 421-3611 Harold Graschuk

Prince Albert: (306) 763-7411 Richard Wilson

Regina: (306) 525-9871 Wolfgang Wolff

Saskatoon: (306) 244-8900 Brian Taylor

Winnipeg: (204) 949-1370 Andrew Bieber

Guelph: (519) 824-1190 Wayne Dunkel

Hamilton: (416) 523-6770 Graham Hoey

Kitchener: (519) 579-2520 John Bowey

Leamington: (519) 258-2927 Michael Marchand

London: (519) 673-6300 James Barnett

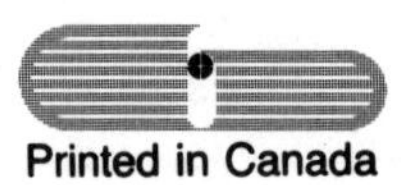
Printed in Canada